Swatc
& Li

C000173464

Also by Maurice Griffiths

The Magic of the Swatchways*
Ten Small Yachts and Others
Little Ships and Shoal Waters
Everyman's Yachting
Dream Ships
The First of the Tide
Round the Cabin Table
Yachting on a Small Income

*published by Adlard Coles Nautical

Swatchways
& Little Ships

Maurice Griffiths

ADLARD COLES NAUTICAL
London

This edition published 1999 by
Adlard Coles Nautical
an imprint of A & C Black (Publishers) Ltd
35 Bedford Row, London WC1R 4JH

First published 1971 by George Allen & Unwin Ltd
First paperback edition published 1987 by
Nautical Books

ISBN 0-7136-5156-3

A CIP catalogue record for this book is available
from the British Library.

Printed and bound in Great Britain by
The Cromwell Press Ltd, Trowbridge, Wiltshire

Contents

Illustrations

Foreword by John Leather

Sailing in yachts and boats takes many forms. Some dream of and sometimes realise the crossing of oceans. A vast number enjoy racing in classes large and small the world over. Many others prefer cruising, most for weekends and holidays which provides a sense of modest achievement within reasonable cost and usually limited leisure. It was for those yachtsmen and women that Maurice Griffiths wrote for seventy years, besides designing small cruising yachts, until his death in 1997. His lifelong devotion to cruising in small yachts, principally on the coasts of Essex, Suffolk and Kent and occasionally 'down Channel' or to near continental waters and waterways, was in accord with the aspirations and experience of most of the readers of the numerous articles and books which he wrote on the subject. His long and able editorship of *Yachting Monthly* magazine, spanning four decades, was vigorous and influential, as he knew well what was possible in yacht cruising for the average owner with a living to earn.

But 'MG', as he was known to many friends and readers, also kept a keen eye on yachting generally. His interest in yacht design began in the mid 1920s when, as the young editor of the short-lived *Yacht Sales and Charters* magazine, he sought some elemental instruction in the subject from designer Fred Shepherd, whose office was close by in London. MG's enthusiasm for yacht design became firmly established from this kindly tuition, and resulted in a gradually increasing succession of generally attractive and always practical cruising yachts; work produced 'out of hours' but much enjoyed and valued nonetheless.

But he most enjoyed being on board one of his 'little ships', as he delighted in calling them, owning, during his long years afloat, a succession of craft which come alive in these pages. They generated not only opinions and cruising yarns which have become classic, but a developing style of cruising yacht in which the ability to sail well in shoal water is allied to seaworthiness, an efficient and easily handled rig, and accommodation which provides comfort and a feeling of snugness below rarely achieved by many designers of yachts. Sailing in them one is impressed by these qualities and particularly by the fact that time spent at anchor can be as enjoyable as that under way.

Like so many others I was inspired when young by Maurice's writings, and he later became a good friend, occasionally met on the coastal seaways and in anchorages. One summer dusk our little cutter stole softly on the dying breeze into the Pyefleet, that quiet creek of oysters and yachts on the north east coast of Essex. We passed half a dozen anchored cruisers including MG's lovely yawl *Tamaris*, lying gently to her cable with lamps gleaming from cabin sidelights and the upflung glow from the main hatch silhouetting Maurice and 'Coppie', his wife, talking quietly in the cockpit after a passage-making day spent punching the short, salty seas of the coastal channels. We exchanged a passing greeting in an atmosphere so typical of what the rewards of cruising meant to him and to many others, including myself – a peaceful anchorage after some modest seafaring – a pastime to be enjoyed rather than endured, all so well expressed in this book.

1999

Preface

Boats, yachts and ships of every kind, together with the rivers and creeks and seas in which they spend their working lives, have held an irresistible lure for me as long as I can remember. Yet no one amongst my forebears of surgeons and engineers and businessmen and their eccentric womenfolk has ever been shown to have had the slightest interest in the sea or ships: my early passion for boats must be a throwback to some remote and unrecorded seafaring ancestor.

Over a range of fifty years I have bought and sailed and messed about in some twenty different little yachts, all of them decked with cabins of a sort and all in length between 17 ft and 36 ft from bow to stern. And through earning my living in the editorial chair of a yachting magazine and by designs of yachts from my drawing board I have been privileged to come into close contact with yachts and other small craft of many kinds, together with their owners and builders. Yacht racing and competitive sailing to win trophies has never held me firmly in its grip: I have generally been content to be a cruising man, and often a lone hand in his own little ship. Amidst the sandbanks and channels of the Thames Estuary and the Southern North Sea I have found all the peaceful joys and the adventures I have sought in my boats. With leadline through the swatchways, spitways or sledways – those shallow and often unmarked cuts between the sands – I have worked my little shoal draught yachts with great contentment, for office ties have made the blue water cruise, the long voyage to islands in the sun, always out of reach.

Some yarns in this book have already appeared in the *Yachting Monthly* and I am indebted to the Editor for permission to include them here. This, then, is a simple chronicle of minor adventures met during fifty years of sailing on the East Coast, both in peace and in time of war, and of the little ships I have sailed, designed, and commanded. It could more simply be called An Old Sailor's Yarn.

Maurice Griffiths

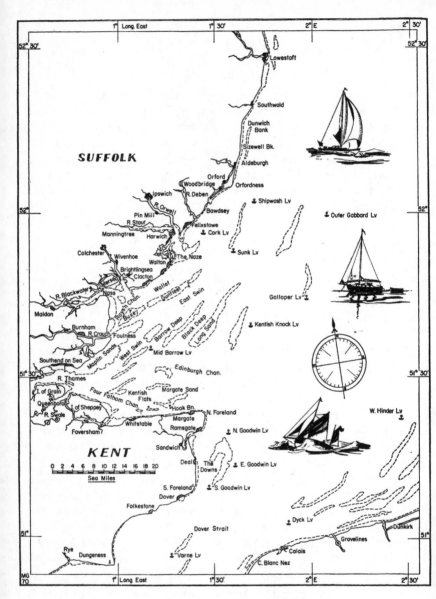

The Thames Estuary and Dover Strait

1 . *Too big a boat*

As evening closed in it looked as if we might well be in for a dirty night. A fine rain had drawn a grey curtain over the wooded banks and was falling with a sad hiss on the still water of the river, and as we drifted down on the first of the ebb the welcome lights of Pin Mill looked misty against the murky line of the trees along the shore.

This was only the second time we had sailed in our very first boat, and we both congratulated each other that this time we had managed to get away from our moorings by the dock gates at Ipswich without even glancing off any of the other yachts moored in the Bight. Furthermore, we had this time set our jib the right way up and had learnt how to work the sheets of both jib and foresail. Happily, too, the light airs from the West had been fair for us and we had not had to make any tacks on the way down the river.

Our newly acquired *Undine* was an old-fashioned, deep- and long-keeled cutter sporting a 12 ft bowsprit with a chain bobstay, wilful ways and a reluctance to come round in stays that was only aggravated by our inept handling. We were thankful not to have to risk missing stays again in the rain and with night coming on and finding ourselves once more on the mud with a falling tide.

When the end of Pin Mill Hard appeared to be abeam a heavier downpour of rain sent us scurrying forward. 'You get the mains'l down,' I told Claude, 'and I'll let go.' And like the beginner I was, I hurriedly threw the anchor overboard, let some fathoms of chain run out over it, made fast to the bitts, and raced Claude, who had by now made a rough stow of the mainsail, to the shelter of the cabin.

'When the rain comes afore the wind,' he quoted above the roar of a deluge on deck, 'tops'l sheets and halyards mind.'

'Oh, we'll be snug enough in this anchorage,' I assured him, 'even if the wind does get up in the night.' In minutes we had the cloth on the table and supper laid and I busied myself with the oil stove and a pan of sausages. Although Claude and I were both new to sailing we had been boy scouts and knew enough to cook simple meals, make ourselves useful, and be prepared – for anything almost.

Looking through one of the portlights my companion remarked: 'There's a big yacht outside going up against the tide. She must have a motor.'

Sailing yachts with an auxiliary motor were so uncommon at that time that I had to have a look for myself. The other craft was a handsome black cutter of some 35 tons and she appeared to be moving slowly up river with a very quiet engine.

'But if she's under way with her engine,' said Claude after a pause, 'why's she got a riding light up on her forestay?' The reason must have dawned on us both at the same moment, for we both made a dash for the cockpit where we jammed together in the hatchway. 'We must be dragging!'

It was as dark as pitch on deck and as wet as beneath Niagara Falls. The anchored yacht's riding light was some way ahead now, still receding in the darkness, and the lights of Pin Mill were no longer to be seen. At that moment our attention was caught by a great round black shape that had appeared from astern and passed along our starboard side with the water washing round it with hollow gurgles. Claude's eyes looked round as saucers as he peered down at the monster and exclaimed in awed tones: 'Great heavens, man, we must have dragged down to Harwich Harbour. There's a submarine alongside!'

I was too helpless with laughter to assure him that the thing was only one of those big ship mooring buoys in Butterman's Bay, but suddenly realized that we must have dragged our anchor unaccountably at least two miles down the river. Claude in any case had hurried forward and was attending to the anchor chain when *Undine*'s keel softly bit the mud and she heeled a little as the tide began to pour round her.

'My sainted aunt,' his voice carried from the foredeck, 'Know what you've been and done? When you let go, nitwit, you got the anchor fluke hooked up on the bobstay!'

My face stayed very red for some time as we moved our meal from the table to the lee berth and settled down once more to the miserably uncomfortable angle *Undine* had assumed in going aground. It would be dawn, and probably blowing hard, before the tide turned and floated us off again, and I had time to think of this first mistake of dropping the anchor in haste only to repent at great length and discomfort.

And during those hours spent lying on our side with the bilge-water soaking into the corners of the lee berth our old *Undine* gave me cause to wonder why yachts should have such deep keels and sharply V-shaped bottoms, so that when they went aground they usually lay over at forty-five or fifty degrees. For waters like the Orwell River with all its mud banks and tricky channels surely, I pondered, a yacht with an almost flat bottom would be more sensible. After all, as far as I had been able to see in my short experience so far, a lot of the yachts on the river seemed to spend a lot of time basking on the mud: and they all seemed to do so at grotesque and discomforting angles like the dead and dying on a battlefield. The thought kept recurring as time went on.

*

Just when our early interests found their way through catapults, airguns, bicycles and railway engines to *boats* is hard to say. While I was at Ipswich School one of my companions was this quiet, innocent-looking but mischievous lad Claude, whose father was an official with an impressive moustache on the old Great Eastern Railway. Claude and I came to share a passion for watching trains – and for the occasional trip on the footplate arranged by Claude Snr – and we ran our own trains on an elaborate model railway in Gauge 1 which we had built up from hard savings and much labour, and which almost filled the attic of my parents' house.

But Claude's two brothers, some years our senior and enviable giants, brought from Harwich a 30 ft smack which they converted into a yacht. When one day as a treat their young brother

13

and I were permitted to climb aboard and look round it was for me something akin to love at first sight. The roomy decks with their sturdy bulwarks; the barrel windlass forward and the neat pinrail at the mast; the roomy cabin in which you could really sit upright (between the coachroof beams); the little brass lamp wobbling in its gimballs; the berths – although devoid of mattresses – on which you could stretch out and sleep; and above everything else the all-pervading tang of bilge-water and rusty ballast, spilt paraffin, paint, varnish, tarred rigging and tanned sails, awoke in me a craving for boating that has not left me after fifty years. I felt as Cortes must have felt when he first glimpsed the blue Pacific Ocean from the isthmus of Panama: that I had been shown a way of life I had never previously thought existed.

Our weekend walks began to lead us more often down to the river where we could feast our eyes on the motley collection of boats which rode to moorings in a bight of the Orwell, between the lock gates leading to Ipswich Docks and the wharf by Cobbold's brewery. Here we could discuss the pros and cons as we imagined them of lifeboat conversions with cabin tops of diverse architectural merits, ancient clinker-built cutters – one painted a dark green with a long counter stern displayed the name *Pterodactyl* which earned many variations amongst the longshoremen – and comparatively smart little carvel yachts of 3, 5 and 6 tons. Altogether in the Bight in those days soon after the end of the First World War there were some thirty to forty boats moored close together, and almost all shared similiar features: they were all gaff rigged, for no Bermudian mainsail had by then appeared on the Orwell; whether cutter, sloop, or yawl they all had long bowsprits stretching beyond their straight bows; there were more counter sterns than transoms amongst the yachts and not one of all these yachts possessed an auxiliary motor.

Sometimes we would find one or other of these boats perched upright on legs, or lying on her side on the foreshore whilst her thigh-booted owner scrubbed her – more often than not he could be found crouched beneath her bilge attending to a leaky bottom.

If we hung around long enough we might have a scrubbing

14

brush thrust into our hands with advice to get on with it, and if our luck held still further we would be invited on board to see the little cabin, feel the softness of the berth mattresses (to me they appeared as though filled with sand), admire the cunning little racks for cups and plates, and note the neat skylight above the little table, how it hinged open to let in fresh air (but who on earth would *want* fresh air when inhaling such a heavenly boaty smell?). For us the spartan little cabin became the most desirable place in the world.

When Claude and I returned to earth our minds were made up that as quickly as possible we too would have a small boat, a yacht. Not just an open boat like a dinghy, said Claude with disgust in his voice, but a proper yacht! With a cabin, I added, with proper bunks and a folding table, and a cooking locker with a stove you can cook on, and – and, Claude added, real port-holes in the sides you can see through, and white sails and an oil lamp in gimbals, and – and, I interjected with conviction, she must have a skylight you can open and at night on deck you can look down and see the cabin all lit up!

But how to find the cash? We had left school and both had jobs of a sort, mine in the office of a local auctioneer and estate agents. There were no expectations from indulgent parents or sympathetic aunts, we had to make up the necessary capital to become real yachtsmen the hard way. With many regrets – for we were proud of our laborious handiwork – our model railway with its steam and clockwork locomotives, its home-built rolling stock and stations and bridges and signals and points and crossings was sold piece by piece together with our air rifles, an old bicycle and other odds and ends of school days, and in time, added to savings from our apprentice-like wages, our joint capital reached £80.

The search was on. But we soon learnt the perennial lesson for all boat seekers: how few craft there seem to be for sale that are anything like what you have in mind, and what exorbitant notions sellers seem to have about the value of their ancient vessels. There was a decrepit old clinker-built toreout with sails in tatters and mildew all over her dogkennel cabin for £100; there was a lifeboat conversion, a topheavy riz-on with match-boarded upperworks for £95; and a smack so wormeaten and old that she had that long-forgotten type of stern with the deck carried aft to a square counter above a full transom – known, we learnt later, as the lute stern. Indeed the old *Ruby* looked like a little Revenue cutter of 1800, and locals shook their heads and told us 'She won't never see a hundred years no more'.

We began to despair. Green but dewy-eyed though we were we reckoned we knew enough to tell when a boat was as rotten as a pear or leaky as a sieve, and the ones for sale all seemed like that. Small wonder, then, when we were offered the *Undine* which we had often admired from the foreshore lying to her moorings in the Bight, our hearts beat faster. *Undine* was a 6 ton cutter with a pretty hull like a smack; a powerful little ship with a full bow and a graceful long counter of the old cod'shead-mackerel tail model, and she measured, we were told, 30 ft on deck with about 8 ft beam.

Once on board we were both captivated. 'Plenty of deck space,' remarked Claude, 'and a fine rail round her.' 'Look at that skylight,' was my breathless comment. 'And the sails are white. She really is a proper yacht!'

I remember the owner gave us both an old-fashioned look as he led the way into the cabin ('the saloon' he called it) and pointed out the fine red berth mattresses, the neat little curtains each side of the rectangular portlights, the useful galley locker with its primus as well as a Beatrice oil-stove, and the neatly concealed bucket lavatory in the fo'c'sle. We looked around enraptured. She was a proper little ship, with her there was nowhere we couldn't go .... I thought to lift up one of the cabin floorboards and noticed a concrete bottom within an inch or so of the boards. We only partly listened to the owner's hurried explanation that the previous owner had been a keen racing man at Burnham and had had that concrete put in instead of adding rusty ballast to help her carry full sail when all other yachts were reefed and lying on their sides. 'They say he had a sideboard', added our owner without blinking, 'completely covered with trophies he'd won with the old *Undine*.'

We did not know then how tired the old girl was after her fifty seasons of sailing, or how soft her bottom was in places. Nor did we realize, when we asked somewhat idly how much water she drew and were told 'Oh about five foot', just what that draught with a heavy long-keeled cutter with a 12 ft bowsprit and no engine would be like for two completely clueless beginners to sail in the channels of the Orwell River. 'She's as easy to sail as a dinghy,' the owner assured us as though divining the direction our thoughts were taking. 'She's the fastest and prettiest yacht on this coast.'

The asking price was £90. Remembering our total capital we looked at one another and tentatively offered seventy. Perhaps we could have read some meaning in the alacrity with which the owner accepted the offer, but it passed us by. *Undine* with all her leaks and uncontrollable ways became ours and our yachting careers began from that moment.

*

That night, when *Undine* came to rest on the mud on the south side of the river below Pin Mill, lived up to the old sailor's saw: the rain had come before the wind and as the first streaks of an angry dawn appeared over the hills beyond Levington it seemed to our inexperienced judgement that the wind was blowing great guns. The halyards were beating a frenzied tattoo against the mast, and one of them, not expertly belayed, had come adrift from its cleat and was stretched out to leeward whipping in the wind like a lash.

The rain had eased off a little but it was still driving across the river like a damp curtain, and as the light in the east grew stronger the scene took on a dreary prospect, heart-chilling enough for the two young apprehensives to climb back into the slanting cabin and close the hatch. But the gale at south-west was fortunately blowing off the land, and when the tide rose and *Undine* lifted on to an even keel once more she soon began to fleet, scraping her deep keel inch by inch over the mud, until she rode free of the ground on the end of her anchor chain.

It seemed all very easy at the time, this floating off on the rising tide after grounding on the ebb. But we were to learn in due course the vital difference between running aground thus on a *weather* shore with the wind blowing off it towards the deep water, and running on to a *lee* shore with the wind blowing straight over it, forcing any boat aground there farther and

17

farther on into the shallower water. The age-old sailor's dread of a lee shore was to be instilled in us at a later date.

As soon as we found ourselves truly afloat on that wet and blustery dawn – only the third of our respective yachting careers, as we were later to recall it – with dry mouths and no appetite for breakfast we fumbled the third and last reef in the mainsail. The stowed foresail was lashed securely on the foredeck, and while Claude below hauled the little storm jib out of its locker in the fo'c'sle I hauled in the working jib by the bowsprit traveller ring. Feeling so stiff that it might well have been made of strong cardboard the storm jib was hauled out in its place.

Winching in the anchor chain link by link with the old-fashioned windlass was hard and slow work, and when old Cold Nose, dripping mud and water, was finally hove up to the stem-head we both sat for a moment on the foredeck panting for breath. *Undine* seemed a big and heavy brute just then. But she had the bit between her teeth and was driving astern at a rate of knots.

'Jib up,' I called urgently. 'I'll take the helm.'

The spitfire jib thundered momentarily as Claude swigged on the halyards, and when our noble steed slewed her bowsprit round to port and headed down river we were both relieved. We had not yet learnt how to back the jib in order to cant the yacht's bow away on the tack we selected; *Undine* herself decided this for us, although at the time neither of her quaking owners would have admitted it. In a mood of propitiation we sank into the cockpit breathless and silent. But not so our ship. With the wind on her starboard quarter beating into her close-reefed mainsail like a giant fist she put her lee rail down and tore through the water like a scalded cat.

'Phew! She pulls, doesn't she?'

I was struggling with both hands and with feet pressed against the lee coaming to hold the tiller up to windward and keep her on her course. As a squall hit us Claude pressed his shoulder against the tiller to help me. It was tiring work fighting that tiller like a hard-mouthed mule, and we were relieved when below Collimer Point buoy we came on the wind, close-hauled our sheets, and found her less bitchy as she sliced her bow into the short little seas. At the time it did not occur to either of us to query whether a yacht should be so hard to hold. In those days it was generally accepted that to be any good at sailing to windward a yacht must carry plenty of weather helm – she should in short have a strong tendency to slew into the wind's eye, like a weathercock. For had we not heard with our own ears one day on the hard an old yacht skipper in a rich Essex voice saying: 'Yew want plenty o' weather hellum so's yew can *feel* her, mate. Whoy, that li'l old *White Heather* over there, she goo like a train she do, goo like a train, an' showin' a clean pair o' heels to all them bigger boats, she do. An' fer why? Because she gits the bit between her teeth, and when we goos to wind'ard she wants two of us 'ands on the tiller, the mate and me together, that she do.' A pause to eject some tobacco juice. 'Plenty of weather hellum, that's what yew want, that yew do, mate!'

That was good enough for our innocent ears, and we accordingly continued to wrestle with *Undine's* wilful helm, not knowing yet how to take much of the strain off arms and legs by tiller lines, although all the bigger yachts that were still steered by tiller were fitted with these simple tackles. And as we thrashed our way down Sea Reach in long tacks and short it also took us some time to find out that with a straight stem cutter (or any boat with a long straight keel) you must not push the helm down too quickly when about to change tacks, and expect her to spin round like a small boat. Nor should you let fly the jib sheets too soon. She must be sailed round, firmly but slowly as befits an old-fashioned lady. Twice we missed stays through our mishandling, coming up almost into the wind and then falling back on to the same tack. Fortunately both times we had left ourselves enough room between us and the edge of the channel to make a second and more careful attempt.

Already we were beginning to realize how little we knew about sailing a yacht, how very much there was to learn, and the feeling that in a heavy deep-draught 6-tonner we had bitten off more than we could chew in our present lack of experience. But whatever misgivings damped our ardour were at once dispelled when Harwich Harbour opened before us, and we could see between the old Navy Yard at Harwich and the end of Landguard Point on the Felixstowe side a line of wave crests that scintillated in the cold morning light like the rounded teeth of a

19

saw – the sea! Cold, grey and cheerless though this patch of our North Sea may have been, for us it opened up a horizon of unlimited promise of adventure, exploration, other rivers, other ports, foreign lands, in fact, the World.

'What about sailing out,' said one of us with bated breath, 'and having a look at it?'

One of the gods who look after young sailormen and children must have been watching our progress towards the harbour mouth and, overhearing us, taken it upon himself in kindliness, before we could sail into worse troubles, to send us a parted jib sheet. The unexpected report like that of a gun, the thundering of the jib in the wind, brought us sharply to our senses, and for ten minutes we were learning quickly the best way to muzzle a flogging sail, avoid the flailing sheet, and get some control over the yacht when she had nothing but her reefed mainsail set. In time we knotted another sheet in place, reset the jib, and bore up before the wind.

It seemed no time at all before we had run back the few miles we had won so hardly, for we now had both the wind and the tide with us, and we raced up river past Collimer Point and Butterman's Bay to let go the anchor under the lee of the trees a mile below Pin Mill. Nervous exhaustion won over our triumphant pride at our exploit as we flopped on to our berths and sipped mugs of hot cocoa, too full of new experiences to talk much.

For the remainder of that adventurous season we sailed whenever our jobs would permit us and made all the classic mistakes. The helpful books for the beginner in sailing that were to fill the bookshelves with monotonous regularity a generation later were not there then; we might have been able to borrow E. F. Knight's *Small Boat Sailing*, a fine little book of the 1880s, from the lending library, but nobody told us about it, and our ignorance was abysmal. Our lack of capital to keep the old yacht in repairs, paint and replace gear became desperate, and we had to admit she had proved too much for us in every way. We realized then how foolish we had been to start off with a boat as big as a 6-tonner.

Despite all the humiliations of doing the wrong thing and being watched by scores of pairs of knowing and critical eyes, the sensation of coming to a stop with our keel in the mud with the tide dropping, and spending a lovely summer afternoon lying on our side while one Ipswich boat after another sailed by, their crews' faces opened wide with grins at our predicament, we had our pleasure out of *Undine*. And one way and another she taught us a lot in a short time. Like all the yachts and smacks and barges in those days when none of them had an auxiliary engine, *Undine* carried a sweep stowed in crutches along her starboard rail. This long and springy ash oar was as essential a piece of equipment, we were to learn, as a yacht's mainsail, and one weekend in a calm a friendly yachtsman who had come to sail with us showed us the correct way to use it. When a vessel under sail lost all steerage way as the wind died, and was in danger of being swept by the tide down on to a channel buoy or athwart an anchored vessel's bows, the crutch would be shipped in a fitting on the rail alongside the cockpit, the sweep slid into the crutch, and standing facing forward you worked the sweep steadily and without haste, leaning your weight on it while you reached aft from time to time to give a touch to the tiller when necessary. By working steadily and rhythmically we were astonished to find how well we could work the old boat along on the tide. You might make only a knot and a half or so through the water, but with a two knot tide under you your rate of progress over the bottom was a good three-and-a-half knots. And taken steadily with no panting or excessive exertion you could keep it up for hours with short spells in between. Many of us learned to bring our little ships home on the flood tide on a Sunday evening's calm from six or eight miles down the river, and thought little of it. For we had the hundreds of Thames barges to watch, using their long sweeps in the same manner. Sweeping was all part of the boating scene in those days.

If by mishap you had no sweep you could tow the yacht rather more laboriously by the dinghy. Our more experienced friend also taught us something about this simple art: how to keep the tow line taut with short rapid pulls of the dinghy paddles, and more important, how to tow with the line made fast to the dinghy's midship thwart, not to her transom, in order to be able to manoeuvre. He explained how a big tug always has her towing hook mounted almost amidships: if the towline led to her stern it could not swing to port or starboard with the rudder, and the rudder would have no effect on her.

The season drew to an end and we decided to part with our wilful old ship. An engaging advertisement in the Yachts and Boats column of the *East Anglian Daily Times* found us a buyer in an elderly yachtsman of experience who sailed round from Walton Backwaters with an old fisherman one Saturday, looked over our ship very carefully, apparently ignoring the unappreciative noises made by the ancient mariner in the jersey and thighboots, and made us an offer so close to the figure we had hopefully placed on her that we almost fell down the hatchway. He gave us a cheque and sailed her away while we watched her go, looking very pretty on the river with the background of trees at Freston. We stood on the shore our eyes misty with tears from a mixture of sadness, relief and downright incredulity. He was a good owner and gave the old girl a complete refit and a new lease of life, and for some years afterwards we used to meet her sailing off the Naze, glad to know that *Undine* which had scared us so often and taught us so much in so short a time was in good hands.

Claude joined two pals in a task they had set themselves in converting a ship's lifeboat into a small ketch, every now and again crewing aboard his elder brothers' smack. On my part clutching my half share of our sale of the *Undine* I started to search for a much smaller boat which I could handle alone if need be. And this time, I told myself, she would have to be a centreboarder that would sit more comfortably when on the mud, and I did not insist that she must have a skylight.

2. *The ideal – as elusive as ever*

AMONGST the motley selection of craft for sale on the Orwell River there was nothing like what I was looking for, and inside my price limit of £40 there seemed not much of anything at all. Prices of boats of all kinds had never recovered from the shortage of good craft after the four years of the Great War.

At weekends and during fine evenings after the estate agents' office closed I cycled round to places like Woodbridge and Manningtree, Walton-on-the-Naze and Wivenhoe and as far as Brightlingsea. There were dozens of small craft lying at all angles on the mud and a few hauled out amongst the big yachts that filled the yards in those days; but all I could find for sale were converted lifeboats, toreouts and riz-ons, or ripe old cutters of 3 or 4 tons, their bottom seams looking like ploughed furrows with a tingle or two here and there, and their deep draught giving them body sections like a mean wedge of cheese – one could imagine how they would lie over when aground. But there was not a single flat centreboarder that could poke into shallow creeks and cheat the tides over the sands or take the ground at a comfortable angle to be found.

It was all very disheartening, and after so much pedalling on a hard saddle I began to feel as ripe as a pear myself and in need of a few tingles underneath. But after weeks of searching I paid another visit to Woodbridge, only eight miles distant, to a boatyard I had not noticed before. It was tucked away about half a mile above the quay where the old tidemill was still being worked from the millpond, and on the ebb tide you could hear the soft fluttering sound of its great wheel. Here the old man in charge of the yard took me to see a 17 ft clinker-built sloop which at once looked promising. She was sitting almost upright in a mud berth with her mast up and all her gear in place.

'*Dabchick* her name is,' he rumbled as he helped me aboard.

'They put this nice cabin top on her for hiring-like on the Broads.'

I noticed there was still a hire register plate on the side of the tabernacle in which the mast was pivoted. Her cabin top was hinged at the fore end, and the old man showed me how it lifted on to wooden struts at the after corners with green Willesden canvas round the sides to keep out the weather, giving good sitting headroom at the after end of the two settee berths. With the rich-looking green plush mattresses and a bucket lavatory neatly concealed by the mast, added to the pitch pine panelling of the cabin doors, the impression was luxurious compared with the Spartan toreouts I had been seeing.

'She's as nice a lil' bo't as you're likely to see anywhere,' the old man's voice rolled on. 'And fast. They tell me she won a tidy heap o' cups racing on the Broads.' All praise of the loved one rings true in the lover's ear, and it was music to mine. 'She's a fine bo't at sea', continued the voice, ' 'cause she's got a lead keel.' The pleasure of my surprise must have registered. 'Yiss, she have. And I reckon the keel alone's wuth as much as the forty quid I'm asking for her, almost.' He let that sink in, then added, 'And she draw only three foot o' water.'

That did it. My hopes of finding a really shallow boat with a centreboard had evaporated, but I thought that with this lovely little craft and only 3 ft draught surely I could avoid running aground. But £40 was my total capital and she didn't have a dinghy or much equipment. It seemed almost hopeless but driven by desperation and the thoughts of the horrible boats I had already seen I started to haggle. To my intense surprise within an hour the old man had agreed to accept £36 for *Dabchick* and to include a 9 ft pram dinghy, a cabin lamp, a primus for the cooking-locker and one or two other items. It did not occur to me at the time that he was used to sizing up young fellows who fall for a boat, and the ease with which he was persuaded could have implied that he was only too glad to get rid of her. The suspicion came to me only later after I had sailed her away.

There were then at least two other boats on the Orwell called *Dabchick* and I decided to chance the superstition about changing a ship's name and called her *Vahan*, a word from Sanskrit meaning a vehicle for flights of fancy. Although it was only January when I bought her I couldn't rest until I had my new possession on *Undine*'s old mooring, within walking distance of my home. Derek, a splendid muscular old school friend of mine and one of the Ipswich Catchpoles, volunteered to help me sail her round to the Orwell one weekend of strong winds from the west and scurries of snow. It turned out to be an eye-opening introduction to the sailing season, for we all but lost her on Woodbridge Haven bar. Under her big gunter mainsail, although double reefed, and the only jib she had, a quite sizeable sail, our boat became unmanageable as she shot out of the Deben at half ebb and grounded amongst the breakers on the outer shoal. Had Derek who was steering at the time not nobly declared that he was responsible for putting her on and, slipping out of his trousers, jumped overboard and heaved her off with his shoulder against the stern, *Vahan* would undoubtedly have broken up, and we should both have been in a very awkward situation.

The ebb held us back off Felixstowe as we slogged doggedly to windward, and near low water close in round Landguard Point we again bumped heavily. This time happily it was only a case of touch and go, and on the new flood tide our little sloop stormed up the Orwell with the bit between her teeth and the helmsman sweating on the short tiller to keep her on course. My first flush of pride did become a little weakened when we found how much she leaked, and how easily she heeled right down to her cockpit coamings under the Broads-type gunter lug mainsail she carried. Indeed during the ensuing months of that blowy and wet summer of 1922 I learnt what a cranky little boat she was, and how hard on the helm. But she taught me how to sail single-handed, and in her I learnt in the best of sailing schools – a boat of one's own and no auxiliary motor to call on when in trouble. With her for the first time I learnt what a great companion a little ship could be, I learnt the joys of sailing alone on an almost deserted river, the cries of the scolding gulls – kiaak, kiaak, kiak, kiak, kiak! – as the rising tide covered their chosen piece of foreshore, the trickle, trickle sound of wavelets under the lands of a clinker-built boat at night, and the crunch, crunch of her bows as she plunged into a head sea.

Derek had his own boat and my other friends were interested in shore pastimes rather than in boats, and I therefore sailed a good deal alone. With *Vahan* on my annual holiday I explored beyond the Naze into the Wallet, feeling as adventurous as if we had been rounding Ushant. A calm held us anchored against a foul tide off Clacton until nightfall, and then by means of leadline, guesswork and Messum's green pilot book *Thames Estuary Rivers* (1903 edition) we worked our way in pitch darkness into Mersea Quarters where neither of us had been before. On up the Blackwater to Heybridge Basin, than to Brightlingsea and the Colne, and thence through the Rays'n – the Ray Sand Channel – into the Crouch and the exciting crowded anchorage at Burnham, we found our way. We got ourselves into a number of scrapes and when *Vahan* went aground on Dengie Flats and dried out she showed me that she could lie over on her side just as crazily as the old *Undine*. Much as I enjoyed sailing in her I was coming to admit that she was not stiff or tough enough for my way of cruising – for I enjoyed the coastal passage as well as exploring the upper parts of the rivers and creeks – and I decided at the end of the season to sell her and try to find a more suitable boat.

Vahan found a buyer readily enough and was taken round to her new home port near Hole Haven on the Thames. Once more by bicycle and motorbus (thundering monster with solid tyres!) I searched the east coast yacht anchorages, with a little more capital this time. Then I met a sailing friend who had bought a 22 ft white sloop with a gaff mainsail and a roller foresail. She was one of the old Nore One designs, a class of small racing centreboarders with a small and very Spartan cabin divided by the big centreboard case. He must have been desperate for a crew for he proposed that we might share her until I found my ideal ship, and for the early part of the next season we sailed together in the *Albatross* meeting both unnerving and merry experiences. Because she had somewhat slabsided bows and little sheer, and was very fast under her large sail area, *Albatross* was very wet on a beat to windward and almost drowned us with spray. Once, after a memorable

26

night aground on the Gunfleet Sands when we came close to losing her and ourselves in a near gale of wind, we reached West Mersea soon after dawn with the tanned mainsail white with salt more than halfway to the gaff. My companion was a fine if reckless sailorman, and it was all good experience, if rough and generally wet and cold.

Then one day I came across just the kind of boat I was looking for, hauled out in a small yard and for sale. She was a white-painted gaff sloop of 5 tons, a shapely boat with a rounded stem and transom stern like an overgrown dinghy, 24 ft in length and something over 8 ft beam. Her rudder had a drop plate to increase its grip of the water, but she was so shallow with her flat dinghy-like sections that with both rudder plate and centreboard hauled up she could float in two feet of water. From a brass plate on the rudder head it appeared she had been built as the *Nellie* by George Cardnell at Maylandsea, Essex, in 1906, and her carvel hull was double-skinned, the inner laid diagonally and the outer laid fore and aft. The cabin with just sitting headroom seemed enormous even after *Albatross*, and there was a pipecot forward in the fo'c'sle in addition to the two settees in the cabin. Once again, of course, there was no auxiliary motor.

Her name at that time was *The Kitten* (appropriate enough, I realized later, with her playful movements in anything of a popple) and the price the owner wanted was £140. When I recalled that all I could raise just then was about half that figure I supposed I ought to shrug her off and forget all about her. But she was very much the type of boat I wanted, she had evidently been hauled out for a year or more and showed signs of neglect, and whoever bought her would have to work hard to recondition her for cruising. A streak of optimism (too much at times) and the reflection that he who nowt attempts gains nowt decided me to go and see her owner.

Both the owner and his wife were sympathetic and charming, and I realized at once why they wanted to sell *The Kitten*. They were both very tall people, he was I think six foot four and his wife fully a fathom (and it used to be said that women were fathomless) and neither of them could even sit upright in their boat's low cabin. They had accordingly already bought a

27

bigger and deeper yacht with more headroom ('I can *stand* in the heads,' said his wife proudly without implying any peculiar habits) and they no longer had any use for the neglected *Kitten*. Our discussion on her (the yacht's) merits, defects and present value was not without its humour, but as a negotiator I was outnumbered and felt a little at a disadvantage when we all stood up, for it was like trying to talk to people on horseback. But we ended amicably by coming to terms that were just within my limit and the little centreboarder became mine to fit-out and launch. *The Kitten* did not appeal to me as a name for a yacht – impossible to hail from afar – and as I was still content to do much of my sailing alone I recalled Kipling's *Just So Stories* and the Cat Who Would Walk by Himself on his own wild lone. *The Kitten* accordingly changed her name to *Wild Lone*.

With this little 5-tonner I found all the simple pleasures I had looked for in a really shoal draught centreboarder blessed with a snug and comfortable cabin. *Wild Lone*'s flat hull sections and absence of outside keel allowed her to settle upright when on level ground, and in her I explored deserted creeks and shallow channels at the top of the Stour, in the Blackwater, up the Colne and round by the Strood at the back of Mersea Island. It was sheer delight to be able to continue to sail on a still evening far up a winding creek long after deeper-keeled yachts had to turn back, and on the falling tide to come to rest on the mud for the night, firmly on an even keel. And it was a delight, too, to sit silent in the cockpit and inhale the scent of the meadows and the marshes on the evening breeze and listen to the haunting cries of the waders working their way along the feeding grounds on the foreshore.

Wild Lone's rig, too, could scarcely have been handier for the lone sailor. The mainsail had roller reefing gear, making it quick and easy to tuck in a few rolls when reefing was necessary – and quick reefing can be very necessary with a flat-bottomed boat. She must not be allowed to lie over on her side as a deep-keeler can, for with no outside ballast keel there was an angle of heel beyond which a boat like *Wild Lone* might not recover against the forces of wind and seas. In addition her foresail worked at the end of a short bowsprit on a wooden

28

roller like an old-fashioned roller blind. Familiar enough to all old-time yachtsmen for some seventy years this type of wooden roller which used to be so common is not often found aboard small cruising yachts nowadays: the influence of the ocean racers has affected the boat salesmen too much. With this fitting the foresail (or jib as the sloop's headsail more popularly became called as cutters grew fewer in numbers) could be rolled or unrolled by a tripping line led to a cleat at the forward end of the cockpit. It was a particularly handy dodge for the small boat, for when the mainsail had to be reefed the foresail could be reefed also by being partly rolled up to any area to suit the balance of the mainsail.

During that season two possible weaknesses of this wooden roller gear were sharply impressed on me. One was that the tripping line must be kept good and strong to withstand the pull of the sheets when the foresail was only partly unrolled in blowy weather. Mine parted one day in a strong squall because the line was a little rotten and needed renewing. The sail unrolled fully with a bang like a gun, and for a few minutes *Wild Lone* bore off to leeward under a press of headsail that she just didn't want at that moment. Happily we were off Harwich with a mile or more of searoom to leeward, and I was able to let her lie partly hove-to with mainsheet eased off and tiller lashed alee while I rove a stronger hauling line and got her under control.

The other source of weakness of this gear was the attachment of the foot of the wooden roller to the metal reel taking the tripping line. The four small brass screws that held the two together aboard my boat sheared off one day in a strong squall and again allowed the sail to unroll to the consternation of her young skipper, and this had to be made a stronger fitting. Some small craft, like the old Orwell One designs, mounted the roller on the end of a boom which was pivoted at the mast. When the helmsman bore up to run before the wind the boom was hauled by its guy to the port or starboard side as required, bringing the foresail with it, and the sail would then act as a small and easily controllable spinnaker. When sailing on a wind close-hauled, however, the aerodynamic efficiency of the foresail was slightly impaired by the thickness of the wooden boom for the length of its luff; but set against all the other conveniences of a roller foresail on a small *cruising* boat, this is, in my opinion, a small concession to have to make.

Were I today called upon to fit a roller gear to the foresail of a modern sloop, or to the forestaysail of a cutter, I should employ in place of the old-fashioned wooden roller a length of standard light-alloy dinghy-mast section with extruded hollow to take the foresail luff. With an upper swivel on the halyard and a large diameter reel (at least 5 in.) mounted on a block and plate bearing at the stemhead or bowsprit, and stainless steel wire tripping line, this gear should work smoothly and not fall apart under bad weather conditions. This roller foresail gear, by the way, should not be confused with the Wykeham Martin gear for jibs. This gear, invented by Major Wykeham Martin in about 1903, was designed solely as a jib *furling* gear as distinct from a reefing gear, although ingenious owners have tried to make it a reefing gear by means of jibs with double-twisted wire luffs and variations of the idea.

Assuredly the comparatively lightweight and handy little *Wild Lone* could be sailed single-handed with great ease. I was pleased to find I could get her to lie quietly hove-to, forging ahead only a knot or so with perhaps twenty degrees' leeway, by hauling the centreplate about halfway up, easing off the mainsheet a foot or two, backing the clew of the foresail to the mast and pegging the helm alee. It made me realize what a much better kind of boat she was for a beginner than the deep- and long-keeled *Undine* with her heavy gear and long bowsprit. This had been a real lesson in foolishness.

Another lesson *Wild Lone* taught me concerned centreboards. Hers was a triangular iron plate working inside a wooden case which divided the cabin down the centre and supported the large dropleaf table. The wire lifting pendant led over an iron sheave at the fore end of the case, up through the deck and aft through the small divided skylight (oh yes, she had a skylight!) to the cockpit. It was easy to operate and seemed to work well. But to get at the part of the wire pendant inside the case and its attachment to the plate for inspection you had to remove the flap table and undo eight screws to take off the top of the case. With this arrangement and human nature what it is, it is not surprising that the plate had not been examined for years, and the shackle joining the wire pendant to the top of the plate had rusted through. One day when we were underway in the Orwell this shackle parted and the plate swung down with a loud thud that shook us as much as it did the boat.

Happily it was a day of light breezes, otherwise the pressure from leeway on the side of the plate hanging down below the keel would at once have bent it so that it could not have gone back into its case. Dropping the mainsail smartly to avoid making leeway we ran back towards the hard at Pin Mill and let go to wait for the ebb to set in. Meanwhile we tried passing a weighted bight of line from forward along the keel until it encountered the hanging plate, and by hauling together from each side of the ship we managed to get the plate partly back into the keel slot. When the dropping tide started to uncover the hard we then towed the yacht with the dinghy until she grounded in the middle of the hard, and as the tide left her we were able to reeve a new wire pendant and shackles and make the case easier to open up for inspection in future.

That was a lesson that has always stuck with me. The short-comings of a centreboard installation which had nothing to stop the board from swinging right down should the lifting tackle part or a shackle become unscrewed seemed to me to be lamentable and to show little forethought. Inspections of other centreboard yachts after that only revealed that nearly all of them lacked any sort of stop, while their cases were evidently badly constructed and invariably leaked after a year or two. It also appeared to me that it added an element of danger to a yacht if her plate could drop right down like that when at sea, for in a flat-bottomed boat like *Wild Lone* the hanging plate could render her helpless, and if it buckled it would act as a big drogue and prevent her from making much way. In strong weather with a shore not far to leeward it could spell the loss of the ship. I began to think that something better ought to be devised, for I learned about then that centreboards themselves were not by any means a new subject; that the first version, a drop keel, was used in the American Navy in about 1789, while in junks in the South China Sea the drop or sliding board, which was hauled up by tackles on deck, was in use long before that.

It was from this accident and from other experiences with *Wild Lone* that I began to take a keen interest in centreboard yachts and in shallow draught designs for cruising in general. Much as I liked her, *Wild Lone* had a number of minor features I thought could be improved upon if only one had the money to plan and build to one's own ideas. But that possibility lay many years ahead, and I went on sailing my little centre-boarder soaking in all kinds of experience and learning something new every time we got underway. That perhaps is one of the many fascinations of boating and sailing in all its forms: after fifty years of yachting you can still learn fresh tricks, something you have never heard of before, and often enough from another who has recently come new and fresh to the boating way of life!

During one of my short cruises to the Blackwater I had seen in West Mersea a very small barge yacht, a somewhat flat and angular sloop with a broad transom stern, straight sides and iron leeboards which were held in to the sides at the waterline by means of angle-iron guides bolted to the yacht's side. This was new to me, and I had to ask a local all about her. Who better informed than Bill Wyatt, the local shipwright, oysterman and punt sailing champion, whose family had migrated to West Mersea generations before from Bucklers Hard in Hampshire after the shipyard there gave up building wooden 'men-o'-war for the Navy. Admiral Wyatt, as the Merseaites called the old man, was a tall spare figure in thigh boots, fisherman jersey and peaked cap and looked out of shrewd blue eyes in a ruddy face above a white full beard. He was always sympathetic towards young fellows with a love for old boats, and he spoke with a local accent that could carry over most of the anchorage.

'Why that lil' ole bawge out there in Thornfleet,' he asked. 'She's the *Birdalone*, one of Mr Tredwen's. There's a lot of them little bawges around the coast like that. Sails nicely, too, and'll float off on a heavy dew, she will! Shouldn't wonder if she didn't suit you, Mr Griffiths', he added with a twinkle, 'if you're lookin' for another bo't?'

But I shook my head, for I was still content with my *Wild Lone*, yet his words were more prophetic than I guessed at the time, for years later on another occasion when I sailed into the Thornfleet Channel, Bill Wyatt was to exclaim 'Why, Mr Griffiths, I do believe every time you bring up in Mersea you come in a different bo't!' And he was very nearly right.

In time I came across numbers of these little barge yachts on the Crouch at Fambridge and Burnham, at Paglesham and round the corner of Foulness along the foreshore off Southend pier and Westcliff-on-Sea. They varied in size from 22 ft by 7 ft beam to about 32 ft with 9 ft or 10 ft beam, and amongst their names I can still recall *Doreen*, *Nan*, *Heron*, *Nancy*, *Dormouse*, *Wavecrest*, *Alceone*, *Vera*, *Venus* and *Curlew*. They all seemed to follow the designs of E. B. Tredwen who had first introduced a miniature barge yacht on the Crouch in the early nineties, soon after the Great Eastern Railway had reached Burnham and started it on its career as a London yachting centre. Tredwen now kept his own barge *Pearl*, a fine 35-footer, off the Corinthian Yacht Club at Burnham, and I learned that he had shown what a small flat-bottomed leeboard craft could do at sea by taking his *Pearl* on a cruise down Channel to the Cornish coast one year, and another year north to the Scottish border at Berwick and back to Burnham, and it was not smooth water or fine weather all the way on either cruise.

The possibilities of these small barge yachts for cruising on a coast like the Thames Estuary interested me, and I decided I would try to learn all I could about them given the opportunity. Meanwhile for the remainder of that season I sailed most week-ends with or without a companion and gradually learnt how to get the best out of a boat of *Wild Lone*'s type. The Ipswich Dock Commission had plans to extend their quays from the Bight down to Hog Highland where the big power station now stands, and all the yachtsmen who had moorings in the Bight were given notice to remove them. A number of the more indignant ones tried to organize a petition against the order, but it seemed to me that Ipswich was clearly an expanding port (it had always done its best to encourage sea trade and the town had offered quays free of all dues to attract shipping up the Orwell as long ago as in the reign of Elizabeth I) and on the principle that it generally pays to co-operate with the inevitable I promptly lifted my moorings and moved them to a spot near the southern end to the Old Channel. This was at the entrance to what used to be the original river bed until the New Cut leading straight to the dock gates was opened in about 1800. The mooring was in very soft mud that just dried out at low water, and *Wild Lone* was a very suitable boat to lie there as she always sat bolt upright and with her very light draught could be away by two hours' flood. Because of their deep keels and sharp bottoms most of the other Ipswich yachts had to find somewhere else where they could lie afloat at low water, and the majority put down moorings either at the entrance to Bourne Creek, half a mile farther down river, or five miles farther at Pin Mill. I used to enjoy spending the night aboard *Wild Lone* at her mooring as she sat still and silent on the mud, and listen to the cries of the scolding gulls and the call of the curlew as they fed at the water's edge. Steamers in ballast would come thumping out of the lock and pass down river, leaving a little wash that would roll along the shore with a sound like escaping steam, and the down trains from London would come coasting down the bank from Belstead, their lights looking in the darkness like a flashing necklace.

Just as I was about to lay up *Wild Lone* on the foreshore for the winter one day I caught sight of a small visiting sloop off Pin Mill which looked so neat and pretty that I had to row over and have a closer look at her. She was a stemhead gaff sloop with a nicely rounded bow, her carvel topsides shone with a glossy pale biscuit colour, and her mahogany transom was varnished. There was no one on board and I sat in the dinghy holding on to her rail for some time taking in all her features. Although there appeared no sign of a chine at either bow or stern I was astonished to discover that she was in fact a little barge, for her rudder had a drop plate and she also had leeboards. The unusual feature about the latter was that each leeboard plate worked through a slot in the deck just inside the footrail and was evidently mounted in a case against the topsides. The arm of the plate was hauled forward by a tackle inside the shrouds with its falls led aft to a cleat each side of the helmsman. It was clear that the leeboards could be left down on either tack just like twin centreboards, and I was struck with the thought of how efficient this must make her when beating

34

to windward, having two plates instead of only one to give her a grip of the water.

Her name was *Swan* and after my somewhat rough *Wild Lone* she looked smart and beautifully maintained. Built as I learnt later by Burgoine at Chiswick in 1897, her hull was double-skin-planked in mahogany with fore and aft stringers instead of frames or ribs – a form of light and pliable construction which was before its time at that date. As one could glimpse through the portlights the cabin was entirely of mahogany and looked clean and charming with its two settees and many lockers. Compared with some of the angular flatiron-like barge yachts I had been seeing, this little beauty appeared on the water as graceful as her namesake, and my heart warmed towards her.

About this time I had met a man who owned one of Tred-wen's barges, a 30-footer called *Curlew*, which he told me he kept on the foreshore off Westcliff-on-Sea. Knowing my growing interest in this type of boat he asked me one day if I would care to sail with him. Would a duck swim! Before I tell you more about the *Swan* and how in time I came to own her, then, let me tell you of an eventful trip I had with Barney in the *Curlew*.

3. *Pause for repairs*

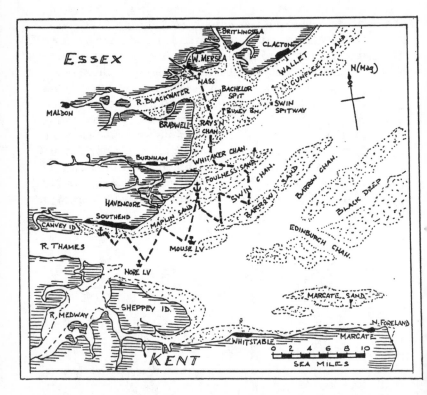

BARNEY'S BARGE was how she was known, and they made an engaging pair together. Barney's cheerful weatherbeaten face and roughened hands belied his calling, for he worked in the City and travelled daily with thousands of others from Southend-on-Sea in the old Tilbury and Southend trains, but every minute he could take off from his work was spent aboard the *Curlew*.

With a high-peaked gaff mainsail and roller foresail *Curlew* was a 30 ft barge yacht built before the 1914 war and typical of Tredwen's designs of that period. With her straight stem, broad transom stern and almost complete absence of sheer a hostile witness might describe *Curlew* as a floating flatiron; but those with an understanding of small barges would see in her angularity a handy and comfortable boat well suited for exploring the shallow rivers of Kent and Essex and Suffolk and – who knows? – beyond the horizon to the Zuider Zee and the sands behind the Frisian islands. Her iron leeboards were hung on a pivot bolt about half-way between the deck and the chine and were worked by a luff tackle led to each side of the cockpit.

Barney's late summer holiday cruise had run out while he and his barge lay weatherbound in West Mersea, and he had to leave her there and return to the office. It was not until a Saturday in mid-October that he was able to get down to her again and I could join him for a sail back to his own mooring off Westcliff.

For one reason and another we were delayed in getting underway at about 1500 hours, and the flood had already started when we ran out past the Nass beacon before a nice snoring breeze from about WNW.

'This is a bit of all right, M. G.,' Barney called as he sluiced down the decks and the water ran musically through the scuppers. 'If this wind holds we shall be able to lay along the edge of the Maplins and dodge the worst of the Thames ebb when it sets in against us. And we'll have the sands close to wind'ard of us to smoothe the water. Boy, oh boy!'

For many years Barney and his little barge had poked in and out of all the shallow creeks and swatchways of the East Coast, and there was not much the pair of them didn't know about tide-dodging and working the shallows. At that time I had barely two seasons' sailing experience under my lee, and feeling somewhat green in the company of such a born seadog (barge hound would be better) I was content to keep mum and take it all in.

'We'll cut over the Bachelor Spit and go through the Ray Sand Channel,' he added. 'It's shorter than going round by the Wallet Spitway, and the tide'll have made enough by then, I

37

reckon, for us to slip across Foulness sand inside the beacon. If the tides weren't neaps we could have gone up Crouch and Roach and through the Havengore Gut, but there won't be enough water today, worse luck.'

As the breeze hardened a little *Curlew* rustled happily on her course, the iron leeboard fussing through the water and the drop plate tackle of the rudder gurgling like a young grampus. With her 8½ ft beam and little more than a foot of draught when both leeboards and rudder plate were hauled up *Curlew* could work into almost any place where the gulls were not already walking.

'Pulling a bit, is she?' Barney grinned at my amateurish antics with the tiller, as I held it against me with both hands and feet braced on the lee cockpit coaming, sweating with the effort to keep the little barge on course. She certainly was pulling, like a stampeding stallion, I said. 'All right,' he added, 'see if this eases her.' And he hauled on the lee tackle until the leeboard was about half way up, then came to the tiller and hauled up the rudder plate also half-way. Surprisingly much of the weight on the helm disappeared, and 'Here, get this line round the tiller,' Barney said, and I found myself sitting comfortably in the cockpit with the tiller line in my hand and all struggling gone. 'The old girl responds to a bit of adjustment to her lee-boards. Most barges do.'

Evening was drawing on as we fetched across the Foulness sands in a welter of sharp little waves and Barney took an occasional cast with his red-and-white ringed sounding pole. He nodded to windward with a grimace. 'Looks a bit dirty, doesn't it,' he remarked. 'Shouldn't be surprised if we get some thunder out of that cloud.'

'Wind's backing, too,' was my contribution, for I didn't like the look of that sky to windward nor the look of all the whitecaps between us and the distant horizon. 'I can't lay better than ssw. on this tack.' And heavy thuds under the bottom told us the weather chine was breaking surface, and as a heavier squall laid us farther over *Curlew* began to gripe round into the wind again, despite all the effort I could make with the tiller line, her weather bow bashing into the short seas and throwing a cold spray over us.

Barney's rugged face was unmoved. 'The old girl's asking us

to tuck a reef in,' he remarked, and in a few moments the fore-sail was rolled up while six rolls were turned in the mainboom. Once more with foresail unrolled with a bang *Curlew* was away still on starboard tack, but sailing less on her side and picking up speed as she drove into the vicious Swin seas.

Rearing and plunging, but with nothing heavier than spray on our decks, we made tacks out to the edge of the Barrow sands and in again to Maplin edge, while the last of the flood tide helped us work our way up Swin. Far away across the Estuary steamers in the Edinburgh Channel threw clouds of smoke across the evening sky, and the tan sails of barges, some with mainsails a little rucked or brailed under their topsails, punctuated the horizon with splashes of colour. With the rising wind in our teeth and the weather-going tide the seas were becoming very steep, and in my inexperienced eye they looked black and angry; and in the gathering gloom the Kentish hills on the other side of the Estuary seemed inhospitably far away. I was wondering what my skipper proposed to do when he forestalled my question.

'We can't lay along the edge of the Maplins now this wind's gone and headed us,' he said in his imperturbable voice. 'The ebb'll be setting in soon, and there's no lee for us out here. It's a pity, but there's nothing for it but to square away, slip back across the Foulness sands – plenty of water for us as it's nearly high water – and bring up in the Whitaker for the night. We'll have a quiet berth under the lee of the sands until low water and we can have another shot at it on next flood.'

It was a relief to have a sure plan, for truth to tell I was feeling a little scared of the Swin and all the angry whitecaps between us and the black sky over the horizon. The little barge lifted her bows over a particularly steep sea as she headed in towards Foulness Point, seemed to hover a moment with her forefoot in the air, then fell sideways into the trough with a jarring crash. Almost immediately there was a sharp thud from somewhere amidships and the starboard leeboard tackle took a heavy wrench and slid aft along the footrail until the parts of the three-fold purchase stretched down into the water taut as violin strings.

Barney acted at once. 'Lee oh, young fella,' he said quietly,

39

putting the helm down. 'Leeboard's carried away, dammit. Roll up the fores'l, and let go the other board.'

Under her reefed mainsail with the foresail rolled up and the port leeboard lowered, *Curlew* lay fairly quietly hove-to on starboard tack lifting and falling more sedately now over the seas. Barney and I sweated on the bar-taut tackle until we had the after end of the leeboard up to the rail.

'Lucky the tackle held,' he breathed, 'or we'd have lost the board altogether.' He got the end of the boathook under the forward end. 'Ready? One-two-six *heave*!'

Together we managed to bring the heavy plate up on to the side deck and put a lashing around it. 'See what's happened? The bolt's sheered off its nut.' He laughed. 'I guess we'll find the nut in the cabin. But not to worry, young fella, we've a spare bolt in the tool kit.'

'What do we do now?' It seemed a good enough question to me in the circumstances, but he only grinned at my expression.

'We can't get the leeboard back in place while we are boxing about out here,' he said. 'We'll have to unroll the foresail again, get her sailing and go about, haul up the other board *and* the rudder plate to take some of the weight off the helm, and stand in over the Maplins, into shallower water, and take the ground on the ebb.'

With her sheets eased and the wind now almost abeam *Curlew* stormed in towards the invisible sands like a startled hare, slewing a little one way and the other with both leeboards up and only part of the rudder plate in the water, but under control all the same. At the time I thought it was something like steering a tea tray and imagined that a keel only a few inches deep from forefoot to sternpost would have kept her from being too wild. It was clearly all right with the wind on the beam, but without her plates the little barge would never have gone about in stays nor made any showing at working to windward. With the starboard board inactive we were clearly crippled for sailing close-hauled on the port tack.

It was almost dark now and difficult to make out even the distant sea wall on Foulness Island, but the white crests flashed across the intervening miles like green fire. And as *Curlew* bustled into the gathering night the Swin seas gave way to the

Maplin choppiness and we knew we were over the sands.
Barney got out the leadline and took a few casts to leeward.

'And a half, one,' he called. 'About nine feet. Keep her going.'

We carried on while the diminishing seas slapped our weather
bow and the tiller struggled like a restive horse in my hand.

'And a quarter, one.' Barney's intonation was as correct and
traditional as the changing of the guard, but out there in the
darkness with the wash of the seas and the staggering motion of
the partially crippled barge it did not strike me as affectation:
like the Ancient Mariner the leadman's call was wholly of the
sea and right in its context. 'These sands are as flat as a pan-
cake M.G. This'll do, we'll let go here. We don't want to go in
too far, as we shall want to be off early on the next flood to get
up to the moorings.'

With anchor down and sails stowed *Curlew* lay rising and
falling over the seas as she tugged at her cable on the first of
the lee-going ebb. And as the water fell lower even these little
seas died down, and by the time we had cooked and eaten a
late meal all motion had ceased, and *Curlew* sat solidly on the
sand with her short mast as upright as a gate post.

The night was cold and we wore our seaboots when we
stepped overboard on to the wet sand which was ridged from
the tide and as hard as a pavement. It did not take us long to
lower the leeboard into position, fit the new pivot bolt through
the hole in the topsides, and screw up the nut against the plate
inside the cabin. All sign of the sea had receded into the night
leaving miles of bare sand, and only a distant roar along the
edge of the sands came to remind us of the boisterous element
we had been recently fighting. The sky was clearing as the wind
began to take off little by little, and here and there stars were
appearing like gems scattered on a black velvet cloth. It always
seems strange to me that the wind so often pipes up near high
water, and then takes off with the set in of the ebb, yet the
weather experts incline to scoff the idea as an old seaman's tale.

As we turned into our bunks for a few hours' welcome sleep,
for we had had a mighty long day since leaving London, some
of the benefits of a flat-bottomed barge yacht were forcibly
impressed on me: here we were, quite still and quiet, upright
and comfortable and unmoved by the restlessness of the sea

that came to us as a continuous murmur from miles away. I recalled the many times in my first boat, the old 6-tonner *Undine* with her 5 ft 3 in. draught in which two years before we had spent many miserable hours aground on our side at 45 degrees with the bilge water soaking the lee settee berth. All the same, it seemed that any barge yacht was very dependent on her leeboards, and if she ever lost one in bad weather she could be crippled for sailing on that tack except more or less to leeward, so that the leeboard fastenings were of paramount importance.

Despite our tiredness and heavy sleep no alarm clock was needed to rouse us when the tide returned in the early hours. A soft lapping of the water, a few gentle thuds under the flat bottom, a slight quiver throughout the boat, and then the sound of scraping under the keel as the water began to take her weight and she fleeted inch by inch across the sand until her anchor chain held her – the gentle sounds had us awake at once.

The cabin clock pointed to 0410 and in the east the first streaks of the dawn were softening the dark edges of the night. Only a light breeze from the west was keeping the burgee aquiver on its metal hoops, but the morning air was nippy for it was mid-October and we put on jerseys, oilskins and seaboots. Far away towards the land, where the low lying wall on Foulness Island showed like a dark line over the grey waters, a raucous chorus told of thousands of blackheaded gulls disturbed by the incoming waters.

With her leeboard and rudder plate only a few inches down *Curlew* stood over towards the deeper water, her tiller feeling sluggish and almost ineffective as it often does when a yacht sails in very shoal water and her keel smells the ground. As far as the eye could see across the still Estuary between the steady lights of steamers the channel buoys flashed and winked white and red in their dozens, while every 20 seconds the green glare of the Mouse pinpointed the light-vessel's position far away to the south. (Years later, with the adoption of the International Buoyage system this confusing light was to be changed to red.)

As day began to spread some colour over the sea and the distant line of the Sheppey shore stood out above the horizon, our game little barge beat steadily up the Swin with the healthy flood tide helping her along. The arresting smell of frying eggs and bacon from the galley accentuated the keenness of the morning air, and by the time the end of Southend Pier slipped past we were feeling on top of the world.

As a cruise this short trip with Barney was indeed of little account compared with the astonishing voyages which have since been made in boats of *Curlew*'s size these days, but we had enjoyed every mile, the yacht was back on her own mooring off the Westcliff foreshore, and I for one felt that I had learnt a good deal more about the handling and possibilities of a small Tredwen barge yacht, and for Barney's quiet instruction felt grateful.

The skipper reiterated the end-of-cruise comment of so many others when he sighed: 'Ah well, young fella, I suppose all good cruises must end sometime. But I wish we were right now starting on a week's potter around the East Coast, don't you? I know this old girl would like it,' and he gave the rail an affectionate slap.

Barney and his barge made a good pair.

4. *Small barges have something*

WHAT weighty dinghies we used to tow astern of our little ships in those days. The old *Undine*'s dinghy was a 10-footer of traditional clinker construction and we thought it none too large for a crew of three. When Derek and I brought the 17 ft *Vahan* away from Woodbridge we towed one of Robertson's sturdy little 9 ft prams, a boat more than half the length of the parent yacht! All that second season I towed that pram around with me; it must have seriously handicapped the little sloop's performance to windward, but I was glad of a big stable dinghy on more than one occasion, and kept it when I bought *Wild Lone*.

There were then no lightweight plastic or plywood dinghies small and light enough to haul on board. The only collapsible boats available were of stiff canvas stretched over a folding wooden frame, quite heavy and not of a good carrying shape. I never owned one but I once saw a friend who was a proud possessor of one of these contraptions jump into it one day from his yacht's counter, and watched it suddenly fold up around him. His expression as the boat sank beneath him and the water rose to his waist made me so helpless with laughter that I all but fell overboard myself trying to get my own dinghy to go to his assistance.

Our anchors were generally of fisherman type with fixed or folding stocks and long shanks and were much heavier than most yacht's anchors today. With no engines to help one haul off the mud or shift one's berth, laying out the bower anchor or kedge was a more frequent occurrence then, and it needed a sturdy and stable boat. A well-proportioned dinghy with a flat section making her stable and less likely to roll over when dropping the anchor over the transom, and a boat that would row easily and carry her way between strokes was something well worth keeping. Good dinghies were rare enough.

Having the little boat behind us wherever we went taught us how to tow a dinghy at sea without losing it. On a sharp punch to windward against breaking seas the little boat might steadily fill with spray and the odd wave-crest, and have to be brought alongside with the yacht hove-to, and baled out. It was when the yacht was running before wind and sea that the dinghy played up. A yacht cannot run faster than the waves created by the wind, and their crests steadily overtake her. The dinghy being towed astern accordingly tends to come along coasting down the face of the overtaking sea like a surfboard, and it can strike the yacht's stern heavily or even in a big sea come aboard and join the unhappy helmsman at his task.

It is in really strong weather conditions that a towed dinghy can become great trial. When a freak sea suddenly builds up astern and its crest rises high above the helmsman's head, and he sees his dinghy poised on the top of the advancing sea just beginning its surfboard run straight at him, it is no joke indeed, and normally calm men have been known to let go the tiller and seek shelter in the bottom of the cockpit. If the yacht does not broach-to as the sea crashes on deck the crew can consider themselves fortunate. Then the boat drops back until the painter tautens with a twang, and the run up begins again – unless the painter parts and the boat is lost to sight.

To avoid this familiar pattern when running before a sea the dinghy needs a small drogue to hold it back. A line from the little boat's transom is usually advocated, and this can be fairly successful, but the line is difficult to retrieve when the yacht alters course and no longer runs before the wind. It has been found easier to control the dinghy's forward surges if the drag-line is led from its bow, as this now allows the dinghy's transom to slew when a crest breaks against it without driving the boat forward. This dragline can be used as a second painter until it is needed, and when no longer required as a drogue it can easily be reached from under the dinghy's bow with a boathook. Other forms of small drogue, such as a plastic filler funnel rove along the painter with its mouth facing aft towards the dinghy's bow and seized to the painter about $1\frac{1}{2}$ fathoms from the bow, have been advocated as successful. When the dinghy overruns, the bight in the painter turns the funnel forward and acts as an effective brake on the dinghy.

No wonder that with no engines to rely on and only a sweep to work at when the wind dropped away to a calm we learned to work out our tides with scrupulous care so that we could make every use of them when possible. With our relatively slow craft we could rarely afford to let any fair tidal stream run to waste. This was particularly important on a passage such as down the Orwell to Harwich and round the Naze to, say, the Colne in light weather. If the wind happened to be in the south-east giving a dead noser most of the way down the river you needed to start soon after *high water* to have the ebb with you on the many tacks to the mouth of the harbour.

Woe betide you if you left an hour or so late and reached the harbour as the new flood was beginning to pour in from the sea, filling both the Orwell and the Stour Rivers; for without a commanding wind you might not be able to work out of the harbour until the flood had begun to slacken. And if you persisted and carried on, when you did make the Naze you would be in time to meet the ebb tide running against you all the way through the Wallet. Indeed, sailing with a strong tide in your favour is like walking up a moving stairway – an escalator or travelator – going in your direction; bucking against the tide is like trying to walk in the opposite direction.

This consideration of what the tides are doing, or may be doing some hours hence at another point on our intended course, becomes second nature to the man who has learnt his seamanship the hard way in slow and unhandy boats with no engine. As the balloonist and the early aeronaut decided their every move in relation to the direction, speed, variation or the complete absence of the wind, so the yachtsman with sail only for his motive power instinctively makes himself aware of the times of high and low water and the directions, and vagaries of the tidal streams: the tides become an essential part of sailing and cruising. Yet today when almost every yacht has what the Dutch expressively call a *hulpmotor* of ample power and dependability this careful use of the tides may not be so vital. No longer is it so common for a skipper when on a cruise to set the alarm

46

clock for, say 0400 hours in order to catch a tide that will start to run in his favour a few minutes after that time, and at once get up and have the ship underway. With a powerful motor that will drive his little ship against most foul tides if necessary, the skipper is more likely to be overridden by his crew – especially if they are his family – who would prefer a few more hours lie in. But even with a helpmotor missing a tide can be akin to missing a train connection: the layabeds may find themselves sailing against a foul tide all the afternoon and end their long day, as so many yachts do, with sails stowed and rumbling over the ebb towards their intended port in the dark. When sailing with skippers like that I find it hard to hide the impatience I feel knowing that an hour or two of vital fair tide is running away while we sit in the cabin having a leisurely meal. There is enormous satisfaction in starting early on a tide, whatever the hour of day or night, and catching the next tide at the right point in the passage and so carrying the tide fair all the way to your next port – and with only the wind and your skill to accomplish it and no help from the engine.

*

My brief interlude with Barney's barge more than whetted the appetite I was acquiring for the small barge yacht, and with the *Swan* still much in mind I decided to ask her owner if he would part with her. Much as I liked *Wild Lone* it had become abundantly clear that a few years of neglect had left her in need of a really comprehensive refit, and I just did not have the money to spare for her. She needed an owner with more resources, or a pair of hard-working partners, to bring her up to full seagoing trim again. When the owner of *Swan* replied that he had his eye on a larger yacht for his growing family and would part with her for what seemed then a very tempting price I asked for first refusal and put *Wild Lone* on the market. Within a week a keen buyer came and bought her, for he told me he had been looking for more than a year for a good centre-boarder, regardless of condition, and this was just what he wanted. With everyone happy, like the ending of a stage comedy, *Swan* the graceful one became mine and I set out to learn any tricks that a small and lively barge yacht might have.

Swan had plenty, and she taught me fast, very fast indeed. I got underway for a sail with her at Pin Mill the day the new owner collected *Wild Lone* to sail her round to her new home port. It was a grey day of moderate but squally sw winds, and as I got *Swan*'s sails ready I watched with some sadness as *Wild Lone* stood down through Butterman's Bay under whole mainsail and her roller foresail, heeling only a few degrees with a fine bone in her teeth and her dinghy riding up on a cushion of white foam. She was a game, tough, stiff little boat, and I was at heart sorry to see her go, but the economics of owning a 5-tonner on a shoestring had proved too much, and a rapid change of craft an answer to a financial problem. *Swan*, this sleek and lovely little ship, was here and needed almost nothing to be spent on her upkeep: we would now see just what she could do.

Following *Wild Lone*'s example I set *Swan*'s mainsail and ran the foresail on its hanks up the forestay, and when she bore away down river with the wind on her starboard quarter I was delighted to find her as responsive and finger-light on the tiller as a dinghy. After *Undine*, *Vahan*, *Albatross* and then *Wild Lone*, not to forget *Curlew*, she really seemed more like a class racing dinghy than a barge yacht of 6 tons Thames Measurement – for I soon discovered that she did not like being left for more than a few seconds, otherwise she would fly round like a tempestuous Victorian heroine, spinning round into the wind as if to say 'Can't you *steer*, you stupid man?' When I tried one or two short tacks to get the feel of her I found her head had a tendency to pay off to leeward every time she was round on the new tack, and one had to learn to use far less helm than any of the other boats had needed, and to check her in time.

Below Pin Mill a sudden gust came down over the trees to windward and in a trice *Swan* lay over until her lee rail was awash and her weather chine must have been two feet out of the water. She seemed to hang like that, trying to make up her mind whether to go right over on her side or come back again, and with my heart in my mouth I clambered on to the weather coaming and held the tiller down with my foot. It seemed minutes before the little minx rounded up into the wind and fell back on to an even keel with a loud 'whoosh'. By this time the

1. *Puffin II*, 6-ton clipper-board cutter of 1897

2. *Wilful*, 8-ton cutter of 1899

squall had passed and *Swan* became quiet again, but I promptly got the foresail down on deck and wound in two or three rolls in the mainsail. In the distance, just hardening in her sheets as she rounded Collimer Point buoy, I could still see my old *Wild Lone* under full sail standing up in the wind like a church spire – or so it seemed just then; it looked as if she gave her broad transom a coquettish wag at me to say, 'Well you sold *me* down river. Now see what you can do with that yellow beauty of yours!'

With the foresail reset we bore away once more and continued our playful gambit together. There was no doubt that *Swan* was fast. As we rounded Collimer Point and tacked to windward down Sea Reach we steadily overhauled and passed two local yachts of deep draught type whose owners considered them – as owners tend to do – the fastest on the river. Their expressions at being beaten to windward by a thing like a barge yacht would have made good illustrations for a cartoon.

Swan was indeed a revelation to me, an indication of what a slender hull with short chines and a fine run at both bow and stern could do in the way of speed. She opened my eyes to the possibilities for fast cruising of the light-weight sharpie type, but it took me all that first season with her to get used to her ways and learn how to get the best out of her.

Whilst she was as handy as a top and quicker on the helm than any other yacht I had sailed in to that date, I had to admit that compared with *Wild Lone* and the other boats *Swan* was undeniably tender: she would not stand up to her sail in breezy weather like the others. Once you got used to this and took avoiding action, as it were – either nursing her with the crew holding the mainsheet, as on a Norfolk Broads yacht, or luffing up smartly to any squalls – she was a delight to sail. Immediately she heeled enough for the weather chine to lift – at once apparent from the thuds under her bottom – you had to ease her: you could not sail her through it as you could a deep keeler or a ballasted centreboard boat. With no ballast whatever at that time, and only the weight of her two leeboards and rudder plate to help her, she relied on her square section amidships and lee chine to hold her up; but because of her fine ends the chines were only about 7 ft in length amidships with a narrow beam of

49

7 ft 3 in. on a 26 ft waterline length. At times before a strong wind with both leeboards and rudder plate partly hauled up she would begin to plane (and almost scare the pants off me as she started to roll wildly). I am sure that given a modern racing rig with balloon spinnaker and a determined and active crew *Swan* could be made to plane like any racing dinghy.

Sailing almost every weekend that my job permitted I found *Swan* just as wonderful a boat as *Wild Lone* had been for exploring to the head of the many little creeks within a day's sail of the Ipswich river. She would glide silently with the faintest catspaw of an evening breeze and find her way into almost hidden pools behind the sedge-covered banks where no other local cruising boat could follow her. Coming into shoal water the sound of the leeboard plates scraping on the bottom was more effective at that depth than any modern echo-sounder, and she could wriggle to windward in sheltered water with the rudder plate up and only a few inches of leeboard showing beneath the chines. But her very handiness made her too much for the lone sailor to manage under all conditions. Coming up to her moorings in the Old Channel, for instance, it was almost impossible to make her lie head to wind for long enough for you to leave the helm and go forward to take up the boathook and reach for the pickup buoy. Even if you first dropped the foresail on to the foredeck (she would sail quite happily under mainsail alone) as soon as she almost lost all way near the buoy the wind would blow her head off and by the time you reached the foredeck there she was with mainsail drawing again, slicing off somewhere else to port or starboard. Getting one's moorings alone was always an acrobatic contest between the playful *Swan* and her panting owner. It was all very well, I reflected, she was a lovely little thing to sail in a frolicky way, but not ideal for a fellow who liked to go off on his own for a time and cruise in a leisurely manner with back against the tiller, or below in the cabin getting a meal while the little ship carried on unattended. Like a pampered girl, *Swan* expected constant attention.

Many years later, long after I had sold her, *Swan* was laid up in Heybridge Basin during the War. During the blitz on London in 1940, I learnt later, a bomb had fallen near the Canal and damaged a number of yachts, and amongst them was my old

Swan, which had her cabin and decks lifted by the blast. After the War she was repaired and extensively rebuilt at Maldon and it says much for her light-weight ribband carvel form of construction that at the time of writing this (1970) I learn that she is still cruising on the East Coast. It was gratifying to learn from the same informant that *Wild Lone,* almost in original form, had also been seen underway on one of the Essex rivers.

The length of life of these two little lightly-constructed yachts has certainly stressed the extraordinary durability of their form of construction, provided it has been scientifically carried out by good craftsmen using only good materials. You will recall that both boats had double-skin planking, laid diagonally inside and fore and aft outside, but whilst *Wild Lone* had light steam-bent timbers or frames (ribs to the poet) spaced at about 10 in. centres, *Swan* had no upright timbers at all, only ribbands or light stringers fore and aft at about 5 in. spacing. I did not know at the time that this double-skin ribband carvel form of hull construction had been introduced more or less simultaneously during the 1880s by several shipbuilding firms (John I. Thornycroft on the Thames, Samuel Whites at Cowes, Herreschoff in the USA, amongst others) when they were building fast steam torpedo boats for various navies in the world. In a variety of forms with two, three or even more skins many modern speedboats, racing yachts and RNLI lifeboats, which demand extreme toughness against concussion, grounding, and a rough life in general, without any excessive weight, this method of construction has been fully developed. Over and over again it has been shown that a wooden vessel, whether yacht, fishing boat or merchant trader, does not last a long time solely by heavy and massive construction. The scientifically constructed light-weight hull has been known to outlive far more massively built craft.

Readers who have been able to bear with me so far will have drawn one or two conclusions, namely that little yachts of all kinds fascinated me, but that I was attracted mostly to those of shallow draught which would settle comfortably when aground. They could also rightly infer that I was not in the least interested in racing round the buoys on a Saturday afternoon hoping to win the trophy, but would far rather sail off into the dusk of a

51

summer's eve and anchor for the night in some silent creek, where the only sounds might be the liquid cries of the waders, the harsh scolding of the gulls, and the sibilant hiss from the tiny holes in the mud where countless creatures expelled their air. Having been born under the sign of Gemini I was forever restless and inclined to seek something else, ready to buy a boat because she might be of a different design, to sail her for a season learning her tricks, and then during the lay-up period change her for another craft of interesting character. It was generally easy enough to change boats so frequently in those days, for there was a decided shortage of yachts of pleasing design in good condition, and one did not have to wait long for a buyer.

At about this time the estate agency business was going through a period of doldrums and two of us juniors in our office were deemed redundant. The loss of one's job then was serious for there were few other vacancies, but thinking that if I could sell and let houses and premises to people surely I ought to be able to sell yachts, I set up in business as a yacht broker renting a tiny room in Ipswich as my office. I was determined that this business should keep me solvent until something better turned up. And it began an interesting period, for it gave me the opportunity to inspect far more yachts than I imagined existed at the various centres around the coast between Lowestoft and Lymington. It enabled me to meet all kinds of yacht owners from those with names well known in the sport to others of a different kind, and I made an acquaintance with other brokers and one or two designers and builders who were patient and very helpful to the young beginner. For a time in fact it seemed as if I had embarked on the perfect way for a keen young sailorman to earn his living.

One of my first clients was a man who called at my office and explained at length what he was looking for, a cutter (no other rig would do) of about 6 to 8 tons. I showed him particulars of a dozen possible boats and watched his solemn lined face as he scanned the photographs with care, but his handlebar moustache continued to droop and his watery eyes showed no enthusiasm as he looked at one picture after another. I took him to see over a boat at Pin Mill, but after half an hour spent looking her over and jotting notes in a pocketbook he turned her down. Another in a mud berth near by, a converted smack, received the same treatment.

'What about the Z—— over there,' I ventured, pointing to a white cutter on a mooring off the hard. 'She's a lovely little boat and she's for sale at near your figure?'

He shook his head, loosely as though shaking his head had become an instinctive reaction. 'No, I've already looked at that boat. She's too old, and she's too narrow in the beam.'

Like the up-and-coming young salesman I optimistically mentioned one or two other yachts I guessed might be for sale in the area, but his head again shook like an automaton, tears from his eyes escaping like raindrops in the wind. 'I've been searching for a boat for a long time,' he muttered, 'but I haven't found anything yet.'

A growing suspicion nudged me. 'How long, exactly?'

'Ten years.' His eyes filled and he looked more despondent than ever. 'I've been to every yacht agent and I've seen hundreds of yachts. I know just what I want, but I've never seen a thing I like.'

A fellow feeling for the other yacht agents and the thought of all the hours and office stationery they must have wasted on this man made my crest rise. 'Look,' I told him, 'in the past five years – half the time you've been searching all over the place for your ideal boat – I've bought and sailed and then sold four different boats, and enjoyed them all. I've enjoyed five seasons' *sailing*. Why on earth don't you go and buy a boat – any of the boats you've seen – and sail her round the coast while you look for your dream ship. Even if she exists, and I much doubt it, you will probably alter many of your ideas quite a bit during the season.'

It seemed to me fair advice at the time, but he had the last word as he left. 'Oh, it's easy for you,' he said wiping away a tear, 'you're a yacht agent. You can pick up boats cheap, and flog 'em to blokes like me. I don't want to get caught.'

Long afterwards I heard through another broker who knew this man that he never did buy any boat, but continued to haunt all the yacht yards just looking over them and cadging questions. All agents, I found, met the inveterate dream-ship seeker now and then in the course of business and got used to recognizing the type on sight. Nowadays, when there is such keen competition amongst the hundreds of boat manufacturers to sell their production of plastic tubs, professional boat seekers are known to rely on free-trial sails for a good deal of their yachting. Some of them, like Droopy Face, never get around to buying one.

My experiences with the fast and lively *Swan* had set me to thinking whether it would be possible to build a yacht which incorporated all the useful points of the flat-bottomed barge with the seagoing non-capsizable features of the deep-keel yacht. It seemed a tall order, but while I sailed her I wondered whether you could move the two leeboards inboard some way, say a foot or eighteen inches inside the chines, and make them fixtures. They would probably have to be longer and flatter underneath and very strongly bolted to the bottom of the hull. A properly shaped iron keel could then, I mused, be bolted on the centreline of the hull in order to make the boat self-righting if ever laid flat. And if this ballast keel and both fixed leeboards were of equal depth the weight of the yacht would rest on all three when she sat on the ground. With the fixed leeboards bolted to the outside of the hull, also, there would be no obstructive centreboard case in the cabin, nor holes in the topsides for the leeboard pivot bolts.

It also dawned on me that with this arrangement of three fixed keels the yacht's bottom need not be so flat as in a normal barge, but V'd 20 degrees or more like a sharpie, and as the two fixed leeboards would then splay out at the same angle it could prove a decided advantage at windward work. When the yacht was close-hauled and heeled 15 or 20 degrees the lee keel would come almost upright in the water. It would then be more effective at preventing leeway than the barge's leeboard or the centreboard, both of which tilt with the yacht's heel and begin to lose their grip of the water the farther she heels. These splayed *bilge keels*, as they could perhaps be called, promised exciting possibilities.

If at that time I had had enough money I should probably have had a boat built by Kings at Pin Mill incorporating these ideas, and risked the adverse comments that would assuredly come from the sailing diehards on the river. I did seriously search through most of the popular boating centres within a day's journey of home, but not one boat with any such characteristics could be found. I little knew that about this time the Hon Robin Balfour (later to become Lord Riverdale) must have been thinking along similar lines in another part of the country, for he designed and built himself in 1923 a revolutionary 25 ft 6 in. sloop which had twin-ballasted keels, twin rudders, a bipod mast rig and other Balfour features. *Bluebird*, as he called her, was a pioneer of the familiar twin keel yachts of today. Some time later, when I was editing the *Yachting Monthly* and had met Robin Balfour, he wrote an entertaining description of his *Bluebird* which I was able to publish together with her unconventional lines in the issue for June 1929.

Before all that happened, however, I sold *Swan* to an entertaining client who brought his family to sail her round to her new home port on the Blackwater. He was a very tall man and his family included two big frolicsome daughters of about fourteen and fifteen who rocked the boat as they gambolled about her decks like enormous elephant calves. *Swan* seemed to sag under their combined ebullience, but they were a delightful family, adored their new boat, and kept her many years I believe until the husbands and babies crowded her out of their lives.

Meanwhile I found another little ship.

5. *Make the tides your friends*

Storm, discovered half hidden beneath a winter cover in a mud berth amidst the saltings at West Mersea, was different from any boat I had previously sailed in, and for a time I felt uneasy that she might prove too slow and poor at working to windward for me after *Swan*'s sparkling performance. For this beamy black-painted cutter was on the lines of a miniature bawley with the same straight stem, generous beam and wide transom stern of this fine breed of Leigh-on-Sea shrimpers and trawlers. She measured about 26 ft over all, excluding her 10 ft bowsprit, some 24½ ft on the waterline and 9 ft beam, and she had a snug pole mast cutter rig. Rating about 7 tons by Thames Measurement she had been built in 1910 at Bundock Brothers yard at Leigh from whose ways so many bawleys had been launched in the past. This yard later became derelict and in due course after the 1939 war was taken over by Seacraft Ltd where many years later some twenty or more yachts to my own designs were built, including my own 10-tonner *Sequence,* as well as scores of other boats.

Like her bigger working sisters – the true bawleys ran to sizes like 32 ft to 38 ft and 12 ft to 15 ft beam, carrying in their heyday before engines castrated them lofty cutter rigs with a whippy topmast like a Thames barge's and boomless mainsails that were partly brailed up when they were 'dredging' – *Storm* carried all her ballast inside in rusty iron pigs and old firebars. Her false keel of oak sloped down from a very shallow forefoot to the rudder heel where her draught was still only 3 ft 3 in., and she was very roomy below because of her great beam and wide cabin sole (or floor). With some two tons of ballast below the floorboards the headroom was naturally limited, but I proudly asserted that I could *stand* under the skylight – well, with head bent perhaps. An innovation in my experience so far was her auxiliary engine, for I had not been shipmates with any petrol

56

power up to that date. It was a single-cylinder petrol-starting but paraffin-running Kelvin giving $3\frac{1}{2}$ horsepower and a speed of 4 knots, perhaps.

With *Storm* began a partnership that was to last, with one break in the middle, for a long time, and I still recall her as an old friend with whom I spent some of my most enjoyable weekends cruising alone or with friends up and down the East Coast. These were carefree days of youth long before the War and I always reckon *Storm* taught me more seamanship than did any other boat I have owned: she was such a reliable, patient companion, like a favourite old black shoe, and took care of her crew whatever the weather. She was so stiff – stiff as a church they say – I never once was able to get her lee deck under when sailing hard, and with her tiller pegged she would remain dead on course for hours on end provided the wind was not on the quarter or right aft, like the good little Essex smack she was. This is an expected characteristic of the long straight-keel boat with shallow draught which makes such a craft so easy for the lone hand to manage in narrow creeks and congested waters. It is not quick responsiveness on the helm that the singlehander needs, the ability to swing round in stays like a spinning top, for with such a so-called handy boat a man has to be within reach of her helm all the time; a long-keeled boat on the other hand, that is comparatively slow in stays, like a smack, but carries her way well, is a much easier and less troublesome vessel for the lone hand to sail, even in the most congested waters. Her progress is more directional: if he is forced to leave the helm to go forward to clear the anchor, unravel a fouled sheet or drop into the cabin for a chart or something, his steady old ship will continue on course like a well-trained horse; she can be relied upon. Extreme nimbleness is an undesirable feature in a cruising yacht. The current fashion to emulate the One Ton Cup and other class racing yachts with a very short keel amidships and a completely separate rudder (in some cases not even protected by a skeg) has produced a race of gyratory boats, many of which have proved to be pigs to steer and to need careful watching all the time.

Storm bashed about the coast between the Aldeburgh River and the Medway that season whenever my agency business allowed me to take the time off. I was at the same time building up a regular connection with sections of the London press with articles and features on all sorts of subjects from boating to railways and shipping and cooking, working as a freelance journalist, and learning by the hard way something of the art of writing. And many of these little features were written and typed (on a splendid relic of a clattering Underwood typewriter bought for £4) in *Storm*'s cosy cabin in the warmth of the little bogie stove.

Another winsome little smack I sailed in that appeared to have all the homely characteristics of my old *Storm* was the Maldon smack owned for many years by the late Alker Tripp who sailed her about the East Coast and featured her, as the *Irene*, in books like *Suffolk Sea Borders* and in a series of attractively illustrated stories which appeared in the *Yachting Monthly* during the 1920s. A colleague had bought the *Irene* for £30 (she was by then a fairly ancient lady), renamed her *Chloe* probably for personal reminiscent reasons, and we sailed her in and about the Essex rivers a few times. *Chloe* was like most of the Maldon smacks – 3 ft 6 in. draught which enabled her to lie on the foreshore below the pointed spire church and get away early on the tide – she was quite light on the helm, and sailed herself with tiller lashed without deviating from her course by more than a few degrees: a child could handle her, although she was nearly 30 ft in length. Years later, after my colleague sold her, she was returning from a cruise to Holland with three tough young fellows in a breeze of wind and a nasty sea. Whether she struck the end of the Outer Gabbard sand or a piece of floating wreckage was never determined, but she suddenly filled and sank, leaving the puzzled helmsman, the story goes, still gripping the tiller and finding himself up to the waist in water. The dear little smack disappeared into a watery grave, but the crew of three got into the dinghy and finished their jolly cruise rowing into Woodbridge Haven.

Like all these little smacks with a straight cutwater and only a false keel a few inches below the garboards raking down to the heel, *Storm* naturally made appreciable leeway when close-hauled, especially in light winds; yet in anything of a fresh breeze she could hold her own against most yachts of her

58

length on the Orwell in smooth water. When she was sailing close-hauled her cutwater would form a small whirlpool on its windward side, and the air from this was sucked down under the keel and reappeared from beneath the weather quarter looking like a writhing snake three feet down. We called it *Storm*'s ribbon, and it clearly indicated the leeway angle of some five or six degrees she was making.

The little chunk-chunk-chunk engine took a lot of the uncertainty out of East Coast cruising and made it easier to work the ship up to the very end of a creek against a head wind. Although for the first season she carried the old-time ash sweep, it got left ashore on one occasion and somehow never reappeared on board, for the Kelvin proved so dependable. The old wooden tops'l and brawny arms days were coming to an end on the river, and even barges with stumpy masts and smoky oil engines were beginning to appear, slinking along like bobtailed mongrels.

This gradual change in the name of progress was not without its regrets. For long years the constant passing and repassing of the tan-sailed spritsail barges, working their tides up and down the coast from London River, and far up creeks in the countryside to pick up cargoes of hay and farm produce, bricks and slates, grain and cattle cakes and barrels of beer, had been a feature of life on the rivers. The outline pattern of their forward-bending topmasts, the cocky rake of their heavy sprits, the traditional furl of their brailed-up mainsails, triced-up foresails and topsails at the cap, which was pricked out against the country-wide skyline as a barge lay against a rotting quay above the surrounding meadowland, was such a familiar sight that we thought of it as a permanent part of the East Anglian landscape. But the beautiful sailing barges were beginning to die one by one. Here and there on the edge of the saltings you could come across a hulk alone, deserted and left to rot, devoid of spars, rigging, hatch covers and paint. And if curious you rowed over to her in the dinghy you might still be able to read on her shapely transom stern the name and the port of registry – LONDON, FAVERSHAM, COLCHESTER or IPSWICH, it might be – and despite the twisted sheer where she has settled to the uneven bottom as though too weary to hold herself firm any longer, her heart like her back slowly broken, you might recognize her as an old friend. Many's the time, you may recall, when this barge has passed by your own little ship, running bravely down river with a bone in her teeth and her brown topsail pulling like a horse, or at anchor with others of her kind under the lee of Stoneheaps by Shotley while a sou'wester blew itself out and they could all get underway together again for the Spitway and London River; or again, you may recall, there she was in the still of an evening with a dying breeze turning slowly up river on the flood tide, the clink-clink of the leeboard winches, the rattle of the sheets and the thrash and thud of the foresail traveller surging back and forth on its horse, sounding regularly across the water as she goes about at the end of each tack.

Gliding silently past your anchored yacht her 75 ft of deeply laden hull, her towering sails, her bob waving lazily at the head of the tall topmast, would seem immense, and on the wind you would catch a whiff of oakum and Stockholm tar, linseed oil and cutch, galley smoke and the scent of many strange cargoes, the unmistakeable smell of a spritty barge at work. The skipper aft at the wheel might take the clay pipe out of his mouth and in braces and battered bowler acknowledge your greeting with a nod.

'Nice evening. Any wind outside?'

'Naw. Quiet through th' Spitway it was.'

'Bound up to Ipswich?'

'Yus.'

'Reckon you'll make it this tide?'

But he is already spinning the spokes of the wheel and the clatter on deck as the barge begins her stately sweep round on to the other tack drowns any reply he might have made to the trite remark.

Ah, we loved to watch the barges at their work, gleaning our weather lore from their movements, copying them when they smelt a break in the windy weather and got underway, or brought up when the tide turned against them and the wind showed signs of failing. There were all sorts of characters amongst their skippers, shrewd, boisterous, sly, retiring, wordless, blasphemous; but they all shared one common feature, they knew everything about working a hundred-ton barge with only one hand to help. The old sailing-barge skippers have become something of a legend now, a race apart and as different from the present race of young coaster skippers as the old time enginemen, whom Stephenson and the railway engineers created and whose like existed for almost exactly one hundred and fifty years, were different from the electric motorman and the diesel locomotive operator of today.

Looking through the faded pages of my log books of those years of 1923 and 1924 I am reminded of several short cruises made in *Storm* when the winds and tides played their dominant roles. One such incident does stand out in memory, showing how important the proper use of the tides can be for the small coasting yacht. The story appeared in *Yachting Monthly*, but I think it could stand retelling with the reader's permission. Here then it is:

A gentle rain was whispering softly over the dark water as we rowed quietly down the creek. Behind us the lights of Walton glowed dimly through the rain, and even the lighted windows of the yacht club were misted from the warmth within. Somewhere across the meadows to the east of us on the high ground stood the old seamark, the Naze Tower, erected it is said in 1720 to guide mariners towards the entrance to Harwich; but we could not see it in the gloom of the night. Beyond the fringe of the saltings the misty blanket of rain hid even the lights of the Naze.

It was late in the season, already into October, and some of the local yachts were already unrigged and about to lay up for the winter. Frank had come down on the London train with his seaboots and kitbag, like the keen sailor he was, and we were about to join *Storm* for a short dash round to the Blackwater and Heybridge Basin. In the dinghy's sternsheets my shipmate pulled his collar up as we rounded the point in the saltings and turned up into the Twizzle, for the night was cold and clammy after the warmth of the train, and I dare say the light westerly breeze found its way through his shoregoing clothes. But it brought with it that disturbing scent of wet marram grass, seaweed and water meadows from over that wide expanse of mudflats known as the Wade. Years after this Arthur Ransome was to immortalize this part of the East Coast in one of his entrancing books, *Secret Waters*, with its mystery and action taking place around the Wade; but we were not to know that yet.

From out of the night my little ship's black hull suddenly loomed large and solid, and soon the gimballed cabin lamp was casting its soft shadows amongst the rows of books on the shelf and glinting on the brass case of the bulkhead clock. I had banked up the bogie stove before rowing ashore to meet Frank's train, and though it was still hot there seemed no sign of light in the fire.

'Better ginger it up, hadn't I?' I knew the bogie was Frank's special delight – as indeed it has always been mine – and when he had opened the damper and gently poked the underside of the fire the chimney was soon giving off a muffled roar and a red glow filled the cabin with a comforting warmth.

Frank tapped the barometer as he changed into his sailing gear. 'Dropped a tenth,' he remarked, his young face eager in the lamplight. 'But it's not all that low. Still, this rain's coming before the wind so we might have a breezy day tomorrow. What's the plan, skipper?'

I had been thinking it over before he arrived, and showed him the chart of the Thames Estuary.

'Look, high water tomorrow at Maldon, that's about the same as it will be at Heybridge lock gates, will be at 1350. We ought to be off the lock by, say, two o'clock tomorrow afternoon, for these are spring tides and if this morning's forecast is right – the secretary at the club gave it to me – the wind seems bound to be a sou'wester, a dead noser for us nearly all the way. My old *Storm*'s not like an 8 Metre on a thresh to wind'ard, as you know, especially if there's a much of a sea, and if we're to make it on the one tide we can't afford to lose a minute of it while it runs fair for us.'

'Then that means a mighty early start, doesn't it? OK with me, skipper.'

I could not repress a smile at his keenness. 'We should have to be off the Naze out there at low water slack – that's about 0630. But it's the best part of ten miles from the Twizzle here and we'd have to allow a good two hours to get there on time even if the wind freshens.'

Frank peered at the chart spread out on the table. 'Then it'll mean getting away about half past four in the morning, eh?'

'If we did that,' I pointed out, 'we should arrive at the outer end of this channel, by the Pye End buoy here, at nearly low water. But at low water spring tides for about half a mile around the entrance there's only three feet of water, and I shouldn't care to risk it with a slight swell running in, even with our easy draught. Those sands are as hard as a pavement, and if we did have to spend an hour or two before the rising tide floated us off we could easily have our keel driven up into the cabin, These sands have broken up more than one yacht in the past. If we wait until there *is* enough water for us over the Pye End shoals,' I added, 'we shall have lost almost two hours of the tide, and with this head wind would never make Heybridge on the tide – if we made the Blackwater at all!'

'When do we have to start, then?'

'I'm for dropping down tonight,' I said, 'when there'll be plenty of water over the Pye End. The flood will be making for a couple of hours yet. Once outside we can bring up for the rest of the night in the lee of Pennyhole Bay, and we'll then be in a good place to make an early getaway as soon as the tide begins to serve in the morning.'

'Good-oh,' exclaimed my excellent shipmate, and we soon had the supper things stowed and the sail tiers in the locker. The jib on its Wykeham Martin gear was quickly unfurled, and as *Storm* swung down stream against the flood tide the tanned mainsail was set, and one by one the withies marking the edge of the Walton Channel drifted past in the darkness. The rain had stopped and the breeze had freshened a little so that our dinghy began to rustle happily as it followed in our silent wake. With the lead giving an occasional *plonk* we sounded our way round the Pye Channel and across the outer end of the sands in seven feet of water. In a few hours, I reflected, the whole of these sands would be uncovered again, and the little black Pye End buoy with its round topmark, which the Walton and Frinton Yacht Club maintained with the other channel buoys for the guidance of yachtsmen into their Backwaters, would be left rocking to himself alone perhaps until next season.

'By the mark two. And a quarter two. Getting deeper.' Frank's sounding broke in on my thoughts and I knew we must now be on the edge of the sand. 'This will do us nicely,' I said as I hauled in the jib furling line and put the tiller down. *Storm* rounded into the wind with mainsail ashake, and when she had lost all forward way and began to drift astern I let go the anchor while Frank stowed the mainsail. We were taking no chances of dragging a loop of the cable around the upper fluke of Old Cold Nose.

Brought up as close as we could be to the edge of the sand in Pennyhole Bay and still afloat at low water we were in a snug berth with the wind anywhere between south-west and north-west. Should, however, the wind back round to the south and blow very hard, we could at once up anchor and run into Harwich for a berth in the Stour or the Orwell. Meanwhile we were all ready to get away on our passage come low water, we said as we turned into our bunks in the warm cabin, leaving the rays of the riding light on the forestay slanting up and down as the little cutter rolled gently in the swell.

With a light offshore wind, or none at all, I have many a time brought up like this off a beach, or under the lee of the sands, for a few hours in order to save slogging against a foul tide and to get a good meal and some well-earned sleep. It is safe to do so in these shoal-protected waters on the east coast provided you always choose an anchorage whence it is easy to turn out, up anchor, and run for harbour should the wind change and come on to blow on shore. You need not fear that you will go on sleeping and allow the anchor to drag until your little ship is ashore: immediately there comes a change in the wind and an alteration to the yacht's motion you are aware of it and awake at once. There is little coastal traffic in these waters at night, but it is wise – I would say essential – to have a bright and reliable riding light. Here you will never be troubled with big ship wash as you may well be if you spend the night anchored near either shore of the Solent, where big ships pass at speed all hours of the day and night. Many yachtsmen seem to think there is something reckless or downright dangerous in

3. *Nightfall*, 9-ton cutter of 1910

4. *Wild Lone II*, 10-ton Bermudian yawl, built 1935–6, at Pin Mill

bringing up off the coast, even in the quietest conditions, and you see yachts motoring for two hours or more against a foul tide merely to get to some recognized yacht anchorage which, when they do arrive, will already be crowded. Tides can be implacable enemies to any small yacht, and it is a wise skipper who studies them and makes them his friends.

The ebb had not quite done when the alarm clock jerked us into life again at 0500. The wind had freshened considerably and the red streamer at the masthead indicated that it had backed into the south-west, making it a dead beat for us through the Wallet and up nearly the full length of the Blackwater. With the sands uncovered just to windward of us and stretching round us in the crescent of the Bay it was smooth enough, and we made a hearty breakfast, cut sandwiches for midday and filled a Thermos with hot soup while the last of the foul tide ran out and it became slack water.

Once clear of the Naze with a reef in her mainsail and only her jib set half-way along the bowsprit, *Storm* began to feel plenty of weight in the wind, but the Wallet seas were only lumpy as yet, for the young flood was only just beginning to run against them. Two spritty barges no doubt bound for the Swin and London River, were slicing through the seas beyond the Naze in good time to take the whole of this flood through the Spitway and into the Thames. Astern of us four more barges leant to their brown topsails as they stretched out from Harwich Harbour. They made a brave sight and would keep us company for some of the passage.

Gradually as the run of the tide grew stronger the seas became higher, steeper and more inclined to break. The wind was now straight down the Wallet and no lee could be gained today by making short tacks along the edge of the Gunfleet sands. The sight of the sand stretching smooth and unbroken almost to the eastern horizon with the old iron pile lighthouse standing gaunt against the sky on the Swin edge reminded me forcibly of the terrible night two of us had spent in the little centre-boarder *Albatross*, when in crass foolishness we had left Harwich at sunset to beat round to West Mersea in the teeth of a strong south-wester against the whole of the ebb. Trying to avoid some of the worst of the tide we stood too far over the Gunfleet sands in the pitch darkness, grounded heavily, and dried out on our side, and spent some miserable hours wondering what was going to happen when the flood made again and the boat started to lift. It did not occur to either of us to light flares and call for help, partly because in those days a little yacht like ours did not carry flares, and all our matches were soaked in any case. In the event we managed to get *Albatross* off the sands just before dawn with cable parted and in a bedraggled condition, but not sinking, and eventually worked our way up to Mersea. The yarn was told in my book *The Magic of the Swatchways* and was one of our most disagreeable experiences, but we were lucky, for these sands of the Thames Estuary have claimed hundreds of smacks, barges, coasters and yachts in their time.

Over the shoals by the Priory Spit buoy the seas became wilder and more confused, but *Storm* doggedly plunged on with the friendly tide under her. To the south'ard of us a fleet of some two dozen oyster smacks from Maldon, Mersea and Brightlingsea were dredging, each with the tack of the mainsail triced well up the mast and a little spitfire jib set half-way along the long bowsprit. They made a fine sight as we stood close-hauled to weather Sales Point.

As the Knoll gas and cage buoy lurched past with the flood tide pouring round its rusty sides I was reminded of another occasion not long before when I had been in just about this spot with two friends in their little 5 ton cutter. It had then been a sharp lesson on taking the tide when it serves. I had joined them, a man and his wife, at Pin Mill to sail their cutter *Wave* back to their home moorings at West Mersea. The wind was south-west with every promise of becoming very breezy indeed during the day. My friends were charming folk but reluctant to get up and get going early in the morning. By the time, therefore, that we had breakfast and worked our way down to Harwich and were standing out across Pennyhole Bay towards the Naze it was past half flood. The wind piped up smartly, and while still under the lee of the Naze we tucked in a second reef and changed to second jib. How glad we were to be of this later!

Wave was an old-fashioned straight stemmer with a very long bowsprit, a lean bow, narrow in the beam and very deep, a type of the late 1880s. In the steep seas of the weather-going tide in the Wallet she made heavy weather of it, crashing her bowsprit into almost every advancing sea, and burying her head from time to time. Even with the spring flood under her she was making poor progress, and as the tide began to slacken our progress on each tack became less and less. How we watched the end of Colne Point, yearning to make it before the ebb set in. But it was no go: the wind and seas were proving too much for the narrow-gutted little cutter to make her way to windward, and by the time we had just made this vicinity of the Knoll buoy we could see that we were merely losing ground. The friendly tide had turned into our implacable enemy. There was no shelter close in to the beach, for the wind was right along the shore, so anchoring until the ebb had run out was out of the question. After a somewhat crestfallen confab held in the cockpit we decided there was nothing to be done but up helm and square away and run back over all those hard fought miles. With leaden hearts we raced past the Naze on the strong ebb, and then turned to punch that same fierce ebb through Harwich Harbour and up the lovely Orwell. Late that night, having had what could in happier circumstances be called a damn fine sail, we were back on the same mooring off Pin Mill hard, and all because we had failed to grasp the friendly hand of our fair tide soon enough.

Today, in *Storm*, we had if anything almost an hour's flood tide in hand through making an early start, and I was about to say so smugly to Frank when he suddenly pointed through the lee rigging. 'What's that over there? Looks like a boat of some sort in trouble.'

There appeared to be a little white clinker-built boat about half a mile to leeward, and a figure in it was waving. 'Better go and have a look,' I said reluctantly, 'In case they really are in trouble.' And we bore away, paying out the mainsheet.

As we backed our jib and hove-to some yards to windward of the boat a second figure in oilskins appeared from underneath the boat's sail and a woman's voice, thin and anxious across the water like the cry of a gull, called out: 'Could you help us, please? Our mast has broken.'

We could see now that the little half-decker's mast was lying loosely held along the lee deck, the sail draped over part of the

67

cockpit. They really were in a bad situation, for they told us they had no oars and we could clearly see the white water across the Coccum Flats less than half a mile to leeward. Something must be done pretty soon if they were not to be swept into the breakers, and without waiting to be told Frank brought our second kedge warp out of the locker ready to heave to them. After one abortive attempt when I failed to put *Storm* close enough to windward of the boat, we got them in tow. It was then a slow beat all the way up to Mersea Quarters with this heavy boat in addition to our own dinghy to drag along, and the tide was almost done by the time we had worked inside the Nass beacon. But there appeared to be no other boats in sight, and as our brave mariners were almost helpless without a pair of oars (why *will* people take small boats to sea without oars on board?) we had to carry on and get them within easy reach of the Town Hard. They were a pleasant young couple and profuse in their thanks.

But of course we did not make Heybridge Basin on that tide. Our best-laid plans had gone by the board, and we had to content ourselves with a visit to West Mersea, in those days less crowded and an even more charming fishing village than it has since become. But if our passage to the Basin at Heybridge had to be postponed until the next day's tide we at least had the satisfaction of thinking that we had lent a helping hand to two other sailing people and perhaps saved them from what could have been a very bad experience off East Mersea beach, if not the loss of their little boat.

They left us cheerfully enough, no doubt with a good story to tell at the club bar. Today I suspect they would have been fetched by an ambulance and rushed to the local hospital for treatment for shock.

6. *Wintry weather on the way*

AN ICY wind was moaning over the deserted anchorage as we rowed out towards our little ship. As I bent to the dinghy's oars, warm enough inside my oilskins and muffler but with lifeless fingers hooked numb around the oar looms, I noticed that slushy ice was forming on the ends of the blades as they left the water at every stroke, and the sack of coal between my feet was already frozen to ice in the bottom of the dinghy.

It was one of the coldest days of that year, and the smoke blowing away from our little cutter's chimney was a welcome sight to us both. Ken had accepted with almost undue alacrity my suggestion to stay on board and keep the home fires burning while Bill and I went up to the village for some more coal and stores, and he greeted our pinched faces as we rounded-to alongside with a wide grin showing his teeth white in a mahogany sunburnt face.

'Welcome back, brave mariners,' he cooed, 'you'll find it as warm as toast in the cabin, and I've got something heating on the stove.'

It was Ken's misfortune that his biennial leave from the tea plantation he managed in India fell during the winter months this time, but he had nevertheless been game enough to accept my invitation to join Bill and me a few days before Christmas for a little trip round to the Deben River, to go into a mud berth.

The cabin of my old 7 ton Bawley cutter *Storm* was more than cosy, it was like a bakehouse; and the red glow from the open door of the bogie stove was reflected in soft light on the bulkhead, the row of books in their shelf, and in the varnished skylight. It reflected also as a square of bright light on the polished brass of the gimballed bulkhead lamp, adding to its own warm glow, for evening was already upon us.

The agony of returning circulation in our hands was just bearable, but it lasted only a few minutes and made us think just what real frostbite must be like, and the proper treatment should we ever meet it, as we settled round the table to one of Ken's spread-out tiffin teas. Outside, apart from an unrigged smack off the end of the Hard, *Storm* was the only yacht afloat in Pin Mill anchorage, all the others lying under snow-dusted covers in mud berths along the shore like a row of cast-off shoes.

The little sail round from Walton Channel had been cold enough with a touch of north in the westerly wind, and a wan sun had glinted for a time on the water as we had rounded Dovercourt breakwater and slid past the ancient town of Harwich into the Orwell. There was a little snow on our decks, and it had stayed there all day, crisp and powdery except round the base of the chimney where the deck was warm from below.

How warm and almost luxurious our cabin appeared as we sat back relaxed and contented after our meal. With a red glow from the bogie and a soft light from the oil lamp there is for me no place in the world quite so warmly embracing and comforting as the cabin of a little yacht anchored in a sheltered spot. And tomorrow, if the wind was not too strong, we would up anchor again and make for the Deben and our mud berth up at Woodbridge.

When one of us looked out before turning in for the night the sky was clear and the stars crisp and sparkling in the darkness, and there was a smell of hard frost in the air that felt like champagne after the heat of the cabin. Even the crunch of the wavelets hitting our bows had a cold sound.

'It's freezing hard again tonight,' Bill remarked as he closed the doors. 'With the glass as high as it is I wouldn't be surprised if we are in for a really cold spell. I hope it doesn't ice up before we get the ship round to the Deben, Maurice,' he added thoughtfully. 'D'you remember what happened to Sandy Cross's little old *Alert*?'

I most certainly did, and shivered. The *Alert* was a very pretty counter sterned cutter built at the time of the Crimean War in 1854, and was to be met all over the East Coast often in company with the *Cleone*, a long lean black straight-stemmed yawl about the same size, a perfect period piece of the 1860s, usually sailed singlehanded by her bachelor owner, neither yacht having an engine in those days.

It was during a hard spell a few winters before that *Alert*, this time on her own, had brought up in the Crouch at the top of high water of a big spring tide. Not long after the ebb had begun to run hard as it does in the Crouch the two men in the cabin were startled to hear a harsh rasping sound from forward and to feel *Alert* shudder. On deck they found great sheets of ice like plate glass floating down on the ebb, a mass of it grinding hard against the bows and tearing its way along the planking.

Working the windlass as fast as they could they broke out the anchor and as *Alert* started to drift with the tide the ice no longer ground past their sides. But it had already cut through some of the planking and water was spurting into the fo'c'sle from both sides of the bows.

Fortunately there was a light breeze, and with mainsail and foresail hurriedly set they got way on the ship and managed to work in towards the shore, where they let her take the ground and lie over as the tide ebbed. It was a near thing, and proved an expensive yard job to replace all the planks that had been cut through by the sharp edges of the sheet ice in such a short time.

*

Morning brought a mouth-watering smell of coffee and frying bacon and eggs from the fo'c'sle that made even Bill stir in his sleeping bag. For a man accustomed to having a minor army of servants to look after him in his bungalow, Ken the Planter was an accomplished and willing cook, and the meals he produced on board were one of the main pleasures of a cruise in winter.

The bogie stove, which had been banked up for the night with a mixture of coal slack and wet tealeaves in layers, was still alight and soon glowing. On deck the wind, a little squally and still from about WNW seemed to cut like a knife when I looked out of the skylight, and the light layer of snow on the cabin top remained crisp and dry.

Soon the mainsail and working jib were set and the mooring dropped, and *Storm* pointed her bowsprit down river as she put the wind on her quarter, bustling along with her black hull

71

turning over a merry bow wave and her tanned sails pressed into bold curves against the grey sky. With her shallow draught and smacklike hull she was revelling in this fair wind with almost the last of the ebb to help her along.

Levington slid past to port with the squat tower of its little church rising above the creek. It was here, so it is said, in the old days the smugglers used to lie low when the white china cat in the window of the little cottage over beyond Pin Mill warned them that the Excise men were around. The Cathouse is still there, but the cat is now only a painted effigy in a painted window.

Collimer Point and the sedge-covered line of the sea wall hid the Trimley marshes to port, while standing up boldly to starboard were the tall mast and water tower, and on the wind floated the sound of bugles from HMS *Ganges*, the Shotley Naval training school. I could clearly recall the original *Ganges* lying at the buoys off the pier opposite Harwich before the 1914 War, with her handsome black hull, red boottop, gilded bow piece, white upperworks, two buff funnels, and masts and yards in the smart 1870s period. Naval ships must have been splendid sights then.

And then came Felixstowe Dock and the seaplane base with one of these tall machines lying to a buoy where now you will find the quays of a bustling, thriving port and a constant stream of roll-on roll-off ferries and container ships.

The friendly ebb was done now, and as we gybed heartily in the doleful sound of the Beach End bell buoy the young flood was already beginning to trickle round its rusty sides. Beyond the dark mass of the Naze to seaward the brown sails of two barges leant sharply against the grey horizon as they stood in towards Harwich with the spray creaming from their bluff bows.

As we lay along the groyne-protected shingle beach at Felixstowe in the smooth water under the lee of the town, the long pier, the prom and the vacant windows of the boarding-houses on the cliff looked desolate and empty; yet in the streets behind the vast red brick hotel that the Great Eastern Railway had built only to find it a white elephant, the shops would be full of coloured lights and holly and tinsel and excited Christmas shoppers.

'Nice timing, isn't it, skipper,' remarked Bill, a pipe clutched between his teeth. 'Tide'll have made at least an hour by the time we make the Haven buoy, won't it?'

Whereas for Ken this part of the coastline was entirely new, for he had never sailed in these parts before, Bill had been this way with me a number of times. He knew how important it was not to arrive too early, or too close to low water at the Bar, or after the ebb had set in. This entrance to the Deben, the Woodbridge Haven, could be treacherous with its shoals and shingle banks, for after a spell of easterly weather when the banks have grown across the entrance and changed the course of the channel, the leading marks on shore could not be relied upon until the local pilots had moved them. And if you were too late on the tide you would face an ebb racing out at five to six knots with a corresponding awkward sea on the Bar.

For the past three centuries at least there has been a shallow and difficult entrance here on which many small craft have come to grief, but in the Middle Ages and back in Roman times the coastline must have been very different. It was hereabouts that the ancient port of Goseford lay, from which round-bellied cogs and nefs with high fore and after castles and a great squaresail set on a barrel-topped mast carried soldiers and stores to France at the times of Crécy and Agincourt. But by the days of Henry VIII Goseford port was no more, swallowed up like ancient Dunwich farther down the coast to the north by the encroaching waters of the North Sea.

'There's the Haven buoy,' said Bill, pointing, 'through the lee rigging.'

We were standing inshore a little now with the great red brick and turreted manor-house on Bawdsey cliffs over the bowsprit end. With the wind still offshore *Storm* was forging ahead handsomely over the tide, and the first of the squat grey Martello towers above the low line of the beach slid by to port. Dancing amid the jobble over the shoals the little black bar buoy was close aboard now, and I overhauled the mainsheet as we came up closer to the wind. The rope was stiff with frost and harsh to the hands.

'Jib and stays'l sheets, please, Ken. We'll just be able to lay in nicely on this tack if we sheet her in well.'

73

'What a place this must be in an onshore gale.'

With a sweep of the arm Ken indicated the rounded backs of the shingle banks on both sides of us. Even with this offshore wind there was an angry little sea boiling around them and giving voice to a sullen roar.

Storm was in the grip of the inflowing flood stream now, and the high shingle beach to port was racing past within a few yards as if we were in a train. And suddenly, like a door closing on a room full of noisy people, all was peace as the roar on the Bar faded away astern and we were truly in the river, and sliding past the few cottages, bungalows and sheds that made Felixstowe Ferry.

'I suppose people do come here in the summer,' mused Ken as he chewed a cheroot, 'but I can't see a single soul on shore right now.'

We shaped our course to leave the Horse buoy to port so as to avoid the wide shoal that nearly fills the whole channel here and catches the keels of so many visiting yachts.

'Look at that sky,' said Bill pointing to windward. 'Looks as if it's full of snow.'

The icy wind was hardening as he spoke. I had been watching that unpleasantly threatening sky for several minutes.

'It looks like being a stinker,' I said. 'Roll up the jib, will you Bill. We'll trice the main now, and put a reef in later if it lasts.'

Blessing the Wykeham Martin furling gear that enabled us to roll the jib out of the way at the end of the bowsprit, I slid along the cabin top, cast off the tack tackle and hauled on the tricing line until the mainsail tack was more than half-way up to the gaff jaws, just as the first blast reached us with a flurry of snowflakes. Under triced mainsail and staysail *Storm* was relieved of her press of canvas and forged happily up river while the wind bellowed at us out of a slate-grey sky and the snowflakes stung our eyes and settled with soft plops into our weather ears. To be able to trice up the tack of a loose-footed gaff sail in quick time like a smack's was one of its great assets in these conditions.

The snow seemed to drive horizontally across our limited vision, for we could barely look to windward, the Ferry had disappeared astern, and to leeward the saltings and sedge grass

74

of the Ramsholt Marshes appeared only every now and then. We were almost sailing blind, but going like a train.

'Lucky for us,' Ken said, 'this lot waited till we got into the river, isn't it? Wouldn't be pleasant outside now, would it. Anyone like a mug of hot cocoa?'

Already our tanned sails were turning white, and the shrouds, halyards and sheets were beginning to glisten with icicles and blown snow. It seemed as if we were sailing an all-white ship through a world of driving whiteness.

As we had hoped the squall did not last long, and as we came on the wind again opposite the deserted barge quay at Ramsholt the wind began to ease, the snow left off except for some stinging small flakes like hailstones, and we were able to reset the mainsail and unroll the jib again. Taking it in turns to go below into the heat of the cabin and warm our frozen hands and feet at the stove, we sailed the little cutter up the winding reaches of the river past Waldringfield – where a friend's converted lifeboat ketch was the only yacht in the anchorage – and past Methersgate Quay through Troublesome reach to the little pool by Kyson Quay at the entrance to Martlesham Creek.

As I looked around at the deserted anchorage in my mind's eye I could sense the place as it must have been more than a hundred years ago with the occasional tops'l schooner working up the river with her cargo of split wood from the Baltic; and every so often grimy bluff-bowed billyboys and Geordie brigs would lie two and three abreast waiting for a berth at Woodbridge Quay to unload their cargoes of seacoals from the staithes of Blyth and Sunderland. And always there would be a constant coming and going of the tan-sailed barges – many of them stumpies in those days – bringing regular trade by its river to Woodbridge and its surrounding villages.

But after the Eastern Counties Railway opened its line from Ipswich through to Lowestoft in 1859 to become three years later part of the Great Eastern, trade could arrive direct from London, and soon coal trains ran through from the Midland coalfields. The collier brigs faded out one by one; no longer would supplies of seacoal be held up in Yorkshire harbours while southerly gales blew and coal prices soared in all the southern towns, the new railway brought it regularly and cheaply straight from the pits.

The sleepy old town began to wake up when it discovered that London Town was no longer a tedious day's journey by coach, but only two hours' smooth riding by the trains; all sorts of things came more quickly and cheaply to be bought in the local shops, and fish fresh from the North Sea arrived daily by rail from Lowestoft. It began a new era of speed and prosperity for farmer and townsman alike.

And when sixty years had passed and the Great Eastern in 1923 became the East Anglian section of the London and North Eastern group of railways, it was the railways' turn to feel the first icy blasts of competition as people took to their cars and the motor buses, and sent their goods by road haulage companies. Like so many other country stations Woodbridge was to become a decrepit skeleton, a sorry unmanned halt of British Rail.

But all that part of the sad story of our railways was still in the future as we stowed *Storm*'s frozen sails. We were only too glad to go below into the warm cabin and to attack one of Ken's appetising meals, and later to sink back on the settees in a haze of cheroot smoke and an air of complete torpor. Outside in the cold the flood tide rose silently filling all the little creeks and gullies, and before we dozed off we could hear the muffled cries of the gulls scolding each other as their feeding grounds grew smaller and smaller.

Bill, of all people, was the first to stir and let in an icy blast from the skylight as he peered out. 'The mud's just about covered, skipper,' he remarked. 'I'd say there's just about enough water up to the quay now, wouldn't you?'

When we turned out, muffled to the ears and our hands in mits, and clumped on the slippery deck in our fisherman thigh boots, the wind had fallen to only a little breeze from something north of west, the surface of the river looked slate grey and still and cold, and the fields beyond Sutton Hoo were a white carpet of snow. From the saltings on the other side of the river there rose a gaggle of duck, and we watched them circle and touch down in a fine gentle dive on to the water amongst a dark mass of their own kind. Their voices reached us like the sound of old women cackling in a market-place. To them the bitter wind, the icy water, the snow in the air were a heaven on earth and their merry cries showed it.

'Up main, boys,' I said as I gripped the steely links of the anchor chain. 'This is the last sail of the season, so make the best of it.'

And we did, savouring every peaceful minute of the sail.

'I'll think of all this,' remarked Ken quietly, 'when I'm back in India with the thermometer near a hundred.'

A small cloud of smoke poured out of the chimney and drifted away across the water to leeward. We were not a day too soon to be reaching our berth for the remainder of the winter, for thin ice had already formed along the mud at the water's edge.

Beyond *Storm*'s long bowsprit lay the rustic seaport mantled in snow. It was here that Edward Fitzgerald the recluse spent so much of his life in translating the *Rubáiyát of Omar Khayyám*, and it was from the little red-brick ferry quay ahead of us that he used to retreat from his too curious neighbours by dropping down the river in his small schooner yacht *Scandal* with only his old pilot friend from Felixstowe Ferry as companion.

As our bows nudged gently against the quay and we made fast for the last time I looked around and thought how little this port must have changed since those quiet days, and how reluctant all three of us were to have to pack up and leave our little smack alone.

As it turned out it was as well, for a bitter January set in that year and in a week or two there were six-inch thick ice floes piled thick on the shores of all the Essex and Suffolk creeks.

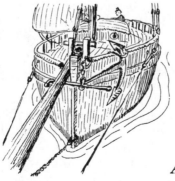

Afrina, 12 tons

77

7. *London is far from the sea*

WHEREAS finding buyers or tenants for houses or office premises had seemed easy enough while working in the estate agent's office, I soon found that running a yacht broker's business was a very different kettle of fish. Not only were there fewer boats available, those that did sell went for only low figures compared with houses, and the whole market for yachts was very much smaller. Net profits from commissions after paying for stationery, postage and the office expenses were almost non-existent. Writing almost continuously in between times I found that I was selling the occasional article to the London press as well as to local papers – while collecting an imposing array of rejection slips from editors – and it began to look as though in journalism lay more hope of eventually achieving fame and fortune than in trying to sell yachts. It seemed a pity at the time, for selling yachts was fascinating in every way, while journalism was just hard and slow work.

My father's sudden death and the forced selling up of the home to pay off his debts (he had always been a jolly and popular man who could not resist helping any appeals, while investing all he had in unwise ventures) jerked me into recognizing the crossroads I had reached in my life. What to decide: to stay on in Ipswich and try to get back into one of the estate agents' offices, or join the staff of the *East Anglian* as a cub reporter and work my way up? Or should I pack up, go to London and try my luck as a freelance in Fleet Street, where I had been told all the best plums were to be found.

For better or worse I chose London (after all, I had been born there, and almost within the sound of Bow Bells). *Storm* had to go to help my widowed mother and her elderly sister and, forsaking any notion of sailing for the time being, I plunged into the dark and lonely world of 'fur. bedsits with gas stove', with my old typewriter, and very little in the bank, but with high hopes.

78

Let us draw a veil over the disheartening struggle any free-lance writer faced then before world radio and television opened out fresh fields for the writer, for after a year or so a little book I had written for the man-in-the-street called *Yachting on a Small Income* led the manager of a new periodical, *Yacht Sales and Charters*, to ask me to call to see him. His name was Bittles and he had just started this fortnightly as an offshoot from the *Yachting Monthly*. The parent magazine had been founded in 1906 by Herbert Reiach who died in 1921, and it was at this time passing through a very lean period under the editorship of an old man who was concerned more with racing and race handicapping than with cruising and small boats.

Bittles had seized on an idea which then in 1925 seemed very promising, namely to run a yacht agency business with its own yachting periodical to advertise its boats for sale. Trying to edit the paper as well as manage the printing and distribution and the yacht agency side was proving too much for him, and when he asked if I would take over the editing and publishing I grabbed the job with both hands, for it meant a regular salary (if very small) and a warm office with others to share. At the same time Dick Faulkner joined the staff to take charge of the yacht broking, and for a time it was a jolly concern with everyone pulling hard together and working long hours. It was not foreseen that this ingenious scheme would put the backs up of all the established yacht brokers who not only refused, naturally enough, to buy space in its pages, but because the paper was related to the *Yachting Monthly* they stopped advertising in the parent magazine as well.

Despite this *Yacht Sales and Charters* rapidly became popular amongst small boat sailing men who asked for more and more of this down-to-earth little ships for the man without much money kind of thing. But because of this very slant on the sport the harsher economics of publishing began to impress themselves on our enthusiasm. The advertisers with money to spend, the big firms, would not buy any space in our pages because, they told us with inescapable logic, our paper did not appeal to the more wealthy yachtsmen with big yachts and crews who would be their main customers. Dick Faulkner shrewdly saw the red light and left wisely to join Captain Coombs, the

Merchant Service officers' friend, who had just founded the Navigators and General Insurance Company. With an ever changing staff we struggled on for almost another year, when the owners of the company decided to combine *Yacht Sales and Charters* and the *Yachting Monthly* to reduce overall costs and infuse more interest into the contents of the older magazine. They appointed me editor in place of the old man, and our first combined issue appeared in January 1927. It was to begin for me a long association with the old Y.M. which was to last until I retired forty years later in 1967.

Before this happened, however, one happy outcome of the struggling *Yacht Sales and Charters* was a letter that appeared in its correspondence columns from a London reader suggesting that there must be thousands of sailing men, people with little boats on the coast, sea-hungry types even with no boat of their own, who might pass one another in the street, or sit together in buses, tubes and trains without being aware of their common interest in boats. The writer proposed that a club should be formed in London so that such people could get together, and he offered the use of a room in the Ship Tavern in Whitehall if those interested would like to meet and see if such a friendly club was feasible.

A dozen of us accordingly met at the Ship in November 1926 and the Little Ship Club was born, and regular meetings were arranged for those interested in sailing and small boats of all kinds to meet over a pint and a snack supper and yarn to their hearts' content. That this idea eventually grew into a club with a membership that surpassed that of any existing boating club throughout the world, with its excellent headquarters in the City, where lectures, seamanship, signalling and navigation classes and many other services were available, was a gratifying realization of a small yachting paper's dream.

Although writing for the press and work on the fortnightly allowed little spare time for holidays or weekends away from London, my old shipmate of *Albatross* days phoned me at the office one day and invited me to join him for his first sail of the season. He had sold the old centreboarder and bought, he told me, an old 8 ton yawl called *Signora*. 'She's a damn fine ship,' his voice enthused, 'You'll like her.'

This seemed too good an opportunity to miss after so many

dreary months without the feel of a tiller. Although walking along the Embankment you could watch lighters working their tides and small tugs pushing their purposeful way through the murky water of London's artery, this only whetted the appetite. Here, then, is the story of that brief Easter cruise:

FAINTLY across the meadows came the sound of the church clock at Maldon striking eight. It was already dusk, and the breeze which had blown so briskly all day out of the north-west, hurrying bright clouds like a flock of sheep across a blue sky, was now but a gentle air drawing catspaws across the smooth surface of the river.

'High water's been gone more than two hours,' mused the skipper as we clambered aboard his grey yawl off the Blackwater S.C. clubhouse at Heybridge. 'We'll have to get underway as soon as we can if we're not to spend the night on our side at the moorings.'

Previous experience of the uncomfortable angle Jay's old boat took when aground lent urgency to our work with the sail tiers. Still in our shore clothes and our kitbags hurriedly dropped into the dark cabin, we had the gaff mainsail set in double-quick time and the long bowsprit pointing down-river leaving our mooring buoy astern nodding in the tide. *Signora* was an old timer of 1890 vintage, 33 ft long with less than 8 ft beam, a straight stem and a square counter stern, and went 8 tons by Thames Measurement.

Jay, her owner, was a remarkable man, big, broad and muscular with a strength and vitality I could not help envying. Although he worked all hours at his business his undying love was to be aboard his boat; so long as he was underway and sailing he was happy. He was one of that admirable stay-at-sea-at-all-costs breed, and reminded me of Lieut. J. H. P. Muhlhauser, R.N., who was later to sail his 37 ton yawl *Amaryllis* round the world. Back in the summer of 1914 – so the story goes – Muhlhauser had set off from Burnham with another Naval bloke for a cruise to Norway in Muhlhauser's Sibbick-built cutter *Wilful*, 8 tons. After several days at sea they closed the West Coast of Norway near Oslo, and without even entering the harbour they put about and started the long sail back to the

Crouch. On the way, somewhere in the middle of the North Sea, they were hailed by a passing British destroyer whose captain, on recognizing Muhlhauser, advised them to make an English port as soon as possible and report to the Admiralty as war had that day been declared with Germany. It was August 4th. Many years later I was to acquire *Wilful*, but never to emulate her distinguished late owner in prolonged offshore cruising! There is, incidentally, a fine glass-case model of the *Amaryllis* in the Blackwater S.C. clubhouse.

'Tell you what we'll do,' Jay was saying with a chuckle, 'we'll sail to Lowestoft and back. If you like we might just look into the harbour, for it's years since I was there, rolling my guts out. It'll be a nice weekend sail, so what d'you say?'

I should have guessed. Whilst my mind had run on gentle sailing with a quiet anchorage or two in familiar creeks at night, Jay bubbled with the idea of making his first cruise of the season a day and night coastal passage as far as we could get in the time. His enthusiasm was infectious but I inwardly hoped for light winds and no hard threshing to windward, for that long winter of 1924 away from boats had allowed our hands to grow soft, and I knew how heavy and harsh was the old *Signora*'s gear.

The dinghy on the end of its painter set up a steady chuckle as the black mass of Osea Island loomed across the skyline to port. One of the channel buoys by the Doubles, a black barrel, slid by to starboard swaying slowly to and fro in the fast-running ebb. There was only one dim light in the fine red-brick house on the island thoughtfully built, it was said, at the turn of the century for inebriates by a member of the Charrington family – perhaps the black sheep. Against the darker shadow of the trees one could just make out the little jetty and the Barnacle, the great post planted there by E. H. Bentall, the Maldon iron-founder, for his big 105 ft yawl *Jullanar* to lean against for scrubbing. Of revolutionary design for 1875 her cutaway hull paved the way for the racing yacht as we know it today.

The night air grew colder as the hours slipped away and the fair tide began to slacken. In silence the white flash of the Knoll buoy drew abeam and dropped slowly astern and the lights of Clacton away to port twinkled against the dark shore line like scattered gems. Despite the faint breeze from the land there was a restlessness about the sea tonight, and a mile to windward of us there came from the Colne Bar a continuous muffled roar like the sound of a distant train.

'The flood's turned against us,' came Jay's voice from the helm. 'We're not making a yard over the ground.' I made a noncommittal reply. Instinctively against the silence of the night we spoke almost in whispers as though fearful the gods might hear. 'Better drop the hook, Maurice. We'll keep the B. B. for another tide.'

When the splash of the fisherman anchor and the spasmodic rumble of the chain had died away the angle of the cable as it grew from the stem roller and the water sucked and gurgled through the taut links, showed clearly how fast the flood tide was already running against us.

We ignored the engine. In the warm light of the oil lamps it crouched behind the cabin steps like a sullen idol, affecting us with a mysterious malevolence. It was an ancient two-stroke of 1908 vintage known as a B. B., and we could think of no better appellation. It had a single tall cylinder like a rusty church tower, said to muster eight horse-power, and carried on its side a snapping contrivance called a make-and-break which was fed from an accumulator. The immense flywheel held on its rim a solid brass starting handle, and when the engine did run this handle whirled round and round like a Catherine wheel ready to catch any unwary trouser leg in its grasp.

For no reason then clear to us this iron monolith when running would suddenly backfire and reverse itself, then back again, first ahead then astern to the puzzlement of the man at the helm, and then stop with a muffled explosion inside the crankcase which rocked the engine on its bearers and shook the whole boat. It fascinated and appalled us, and it was only the following winter when an understanding engineer took the cylinder off that the cause came to light. Whoever had last assembled the monster had put the ridged piston the wrong way round, so that hot exhaust gases were encouraged to explode the incoming mixture from the crankcase instead of escaping in good time through the exhaust ports.

'The petrol tank's empty anyway,' remarked Jay with a touch

of relief in his voice. 'I expect old Fred forgot to fill it for me. We'll have to buy some when we get ashore at Lowestoft.'

There was also another discovery I had just made revealing old Fred the caretaker's forgetfulness.

'There's only about a gallon in the water breaker,' I said, after sounding the fat oval-sectioned barrel on the after deck.

'It's the colour of coffee and must be last year's water.'

Jay's ruddy face lost none of its expression of happiness.

'Oh there's some left in the kettle,' he said cheerfully. 'It's probably been there since I laid up, but we can make do till we get ashore somewhere to fill up.'

I have thought that there must be something a little mad about all those of us who voluntarily go to sea in little ships for pleasure.

*

All next day light airs from the east alternated with a glassy calm. We set everything we had in the sail locker, main topsail, the second jib as a jibtopsail, and a light foresail as a mizzen staysail, but *Signora*'s progress towards Lowestoft, past the Naze and Felixstowe, the wooded cliffs at Bawdsey and the hidden entrance to the Orford Haven, continued slow and painstaking.

Like a striped column on the broad promontory past Shinglestreet, the Orfordness lighthouse drew slowly abeam, and in the quiet of the evening the old yawl hung motionless against the last of the flood tide a cable's length off Aldeburgh beach. Our brackish water was all gone and the juice from a tin of pineapple did little to ease our thirst. Besides, without petrol in the tank the sullen monster beneath the cabin steps was useless should we suddenly have need of it.

The anchor was let go with a heavy splash and the sails stowed. Sounds drifted out from the shore, people's voices, a dog barking, the rhythmic wash of the gentle swell along the shingle beach, while the sun sank lower towards the flat Suffolk hills.

Almost unnoticed, a change was coming over the weather. In place of the hot sunshine and cloudless sky of the day, a hard bank of cloud was making up over the horizon to the westward like a black jagged wall.

'Don't like the look of that,' Jay remarked as we put the cans in the dinghy. 'The glass has fallen, too. We'll get our water and petrol and see what the night brings.'

Hauled up high on the beach stood a row of what looked like black and white striped beach huts on cartwheels. Quaint and little altered since the day that van Tromp sailed past on his way to the Downs in his fleet of high-sterned Dutch warships, Aldeburgh at the date of our visit was still one of the last English seaside towns to cling to the propriety of the old-fashioned bathing machines. And the capstans for hauling the fishing boats up the steep beach seemed in much the same positions as those shown on a fine engraving of *Aldboro* dated 1594 which could at one time be seen in the little Moot Hall.

*

True to the promise in the sky and the falling barometer, when the alarm clock dragged us out of our warm bunks at 0300 a patter of rain on deck heralded smart gusts that set the halyards to thrashing the masts. It was dead low water and still very dark as we hove up the anchor and got underway with jib and reefed main. The wind was wsw, just enough off shore for us to lay close to the five-second flash of Orfordness light; and it brought with it from across the Slaughden marshes the fresh scent of wet meadows and marram grass.

Steaming mugs of cocoa passed up through the hatch helped to keep out the cold as dawn spread with an unhealthy yellow glow across the horizon, and the shapes of the waves began to show themselves against the dark restlessness of the sea. Away from the lee of the Ness *Signora* lay down to the rising squalls, burying her lee rail in dark water, her rigging thrumming in the wind, her lean bows plunging and rearing over the seas with the water cascading over the foredeck. How glad we now were of the skipper's caution in getting in a reef while still at anchor. In this welter of a dead noser and weather-going tide *Signora* would have been unmanageable with staysail and mizzen set.

'Good job we didn't get to Lowestoft after all,' said the skipper

85

as he braced himself in his streaming oilskins, a foot against the lee cockpit coaming, a taut line around the tiller, and a happy grin on his face beneath an ear-protecting woollen cap. 'The old girl does pull a bit, doesn't she.'

She certainly did, like so many of the old yachts of her kind when close-hauled in this weight of wind. Without tiller lines the helmsman would have had to wrestle with both hands and feet to hold her from slewing into the wind; steering would have been hard labour to him. But *Signora*'s owner knew all about holding a hard-mouthed boat without straining himself.

'Ready about.'

Watching for a smooth patch amongst the tumbling crests ahead he started to put the helm down, just a little at first until the bows began to round up into the wind, then firmly down to the lee coaming. As soon as the jib began to quiver – not a moment before – I let fly from the cleat as her head lifted over a sea and her long bowsprit stabbed the sky, then in sheet and belay smartly before the jib had time to fill on the new tack. Getting one of these old-timers about in a seaway with their long keels and bowsprits called for understanding and team-work. I have sometimes wondered what some of today's Sunday sailors would make of a straight-stemmer like *Signora*.

The old yawl's bow lifted over a lumping sea and fell, burying her bowsprit in the next comber with a crash, then staggered upward again with the spar whipping under the weight of spray in the jib. No wonder the old lean-bowed yachts used to lose their bowsprits in seas like this.

'Too much of a good thing, this!' The skipper evidently shouted his remark, but I could only just hear him above the roar of the wind in my sou'wester. 'We'll haul that weather jibsheet in, get her hove-to, and tuck in another reef.'

While the ship lay quiet enough we wrestled with the main toppinglift, halyards, reef tackle and then reef points.

We were still under the partial lee of the Ness and the seas were not yet so steep and vicious as they undoubtedly would be once we drew away from the shingle bank. Jay took a quick look around at the sky as we sweated up the peak again.

'While we're about it,' he said, 'I think we'll have that jib down and set the stays'l instead. It looks as though it could blow harder, and the old girl will be much easier with that rig. Come on, jib halyards!'

His bulky form seemed to fill the pitching foredeck as he muzzled the wildly flogging jib as I eased away on the halyard. Once the sail was stowed and lashed securely to the bowsprit we set the forestaysail, hauled in the mainsheet, cast off the tiller line, and let her go again.

The effect of this snug all-inboard rig – double-reefed main and working staysail – was enlightening. *Signora* had changed from a hard-mouthed old harridan into a far more ladylike boat; her lee rail was only every now and then washed down instead of wallowing under tons of water, and the lighter pull on the helm showed she was under better balance. Without being so hard pressed she was presenting a better shape to drive through the water, and the smaller angle of the tiller meant that the rudder was causing less drag. Instead of staggering along with her lee deck full of water, dropping twice into the same hollows, she was driving ahead all the time with the young flood tide under her lee bow. Knowing from trial and error just what combination of sails any boat likes best is half-way towards keeping control of her when conditions get really bad at sea. On this occasion we were to be glad my Skipper had wisely sent the big jib down and got his ship under snug canvas before we started punching into the nasty seas clear of the Ness.

Bound as we now were to the southward and home there were no good easy harbours to run into until we should fetch Harwich. Round the Ness a few miles farther on the entrance to the Orford River was a mass of white water over its tricky shingle bar, and no place for a boat of *Signora*'s 5½ ft draught today. Six miles farther on Woodbridge Haven bar would not be much better, as it could have altered completely since we had looked in there the previous summer. There was nothing for it but to press on until we could make Harwich, or if any gear parted or sails blew away in extreme conditions (we half expected anything to happen, for the barometer had fallen five tenths) we should be forced to turn tail and run back for Lowestoft.

Only one other vessel was in sight. Under topsail, foresail and mizzen, with her mainsail brailed up a barge was running steadily past a mile to seaward, most likely bound for Gorleston and Yarmouth. Over the tops of the racing seas the fulsome curves of her tanned sails – for we could scarcely see her deep-laden hull – looked a fine sight and our hearts warmed towards her and her kind.

Along the shingle shoreline the seas were a broken mass of white with a fine mist of spray driving inland like steam. Above the shouting of the wind in our rigging we could hear their sullen roar, a chilling sound when you are slogging hard to windward along an unfriendly coast. But the old yawl was giving us confidence as she reared and plunged her way to windward, the embodiment of grace and power; and steadily she gained the slight lee of the Naze, eased sheets; and like an old lady picking up her skirts to hurry in out of the rain, stormed into the smoother waters of Harwich Harbour.

With our eyes rimmed with salt and our hands smarting from hauling on the sheets, I for one was glad to leave the wet turmoil of the North Sea behind and look for a snug berth under the lee of Stone Heaps on the Shotley side of the Orwell. We let go amongst a group of six spritty barges which were also sheltering from the weather. And that night it did blow great guns from the south-west, and as we looked out at the barges' riding lights swaying in the gusts we were thankful we were not out there somewhere off the Suffolk coast.

*

By next forenoon the sharp little gale had blown itself out, and when the wind veered little by little towards the north-west and the grey sky began to break up into hurrying clouds with patches of deep blue, one after the other the barges' anchors were hove up to the merry *clink-clink* sound of their windlasses, topsails hoisted to the truck, mainsails unbrailed, staysails set, and the graceful vessels stood out towards the sea to catch the first of the flood tide on their way to London River.

Following their example we too got underway and stood out towards the Naze under our four lowers with reefs shaken out, taking the last of the ebb across Pennyhole Bay. The sea was a sandy green today, quiet and friendly, as though it would never be anything else, and the sandstone cliffs of Walton, Frinton and Clacton as they passed by in turn looked friendly, too, as the flood tide helped us on our way. It is surely one of the enticing things about sailing in boats that no two days are exactly alike, that in having to take the rough with the smooth you learn a tolerance and humility for man's frailty in the face of the elements that no one could learn on shore.

Later that day, when *Signora* was once more on her mooring off the Heybridge clubhouse and we were reluctantly packing our gear ready to join the weekend holidaymakers on the train for London, Jay wrapped up the story of our little cruise in a nutshell.

'Well, if we didn't get anywhere in particular,' he beamed, 'we've at least got back to our moorings on the tide. And, let's face it, we've had a damn fine sail, haven't we old chap!'

Who could but agree? And when he added, 'You've been working too hard, Maurice, and you really ought to take a little break. What about signing on for a whole week next month and see if we can't get the old *Signora* over to Holland and back. What say?' I said it. Although I had sailed my *Storm* frequently between Aldeburgh and the Thames, I had never been across to the Other Side, been foreign as the bargees said, and this would be a fine chance with a good skipper for some experience.

I was to get it.

8. *There's always a first time*

IT WAS already dusk and the great cranes on the quay were silhouetted like gaunt skeletons against the swaying harbour lights when the skipper came back on board.

'I've been up to the Harbourmaster's office,' he told me as he settled on the starboard settee, his ruddy face glowing in the lamplight with anticipation. I surely recognized the expression: it meant that we were going to put to sea come what may. 'They think this sou'westerly wind will probably blow itself out in an hour or two, and we might be able to fetch across in reasonable conditions.' He pulled Stanford's coloured chart of the Southern North Sea from its rack and spread it out on the table. 'In case it falls right away and leaves us slopping about in the middle of the North Sea are you game to make a dash for it tonight?'

After lying cooped up in port for two long days by a strong SW wind any sort of activity – even a departure on such a night – seemed better than the tedium of dockside Vlissingen. I knew that Jay, my skipper and *Signora*'s owner, just had to be back in his office in 48 hours' time, and a forced passage back to the Blackwater river where he kept his old 8 ton yawl would have to be attempted, whatever the conditions. This was in the days long before there were any air services and good yacht harbours, and Jay was not the kind of owner who could return home on the night boat to Parkeston leaving his beloved little ship in a dirty foreign port.

'All right, young feller-me-lad,' he said finally, 'will you tuck a reef in the mains'l and put stops on the Wykeham Martin jib – oh, and lash the cover over the forehatch – while I cook some supper. No sense in going to sea on empty stomachs, is there?'

90

It was blowy on deck with dust swirling off the quayside, and I wondered how right the harbour officials might be in telling us the wind would drop away. Regular weather forecasts on the air were still in the future, and in any case we had no bulky wireless set aboard the *Signora*. By the time I had carried out skipper's orders and snugged down on deck there were bowls of porridge, bread and butter and jam, and a big pot of tea on the table. It was Jay's custom before starting on a passage to have a large bowl of hot porridge with brown sugar, and to this day I know of nothing better to put confidence as well as bulk inside a man and make him less likely to be sea-sick.

As the *Signora* poked her long bowsprit and straight stem into the dark Scheldt, feeling the ebb under her lee bow, she tacked out towards the Spleet Channel, the dark water washing in through the lee scuppers and her tanned sails curtseying eerily against a black starless sky. The wind seemed to moan in the rigging with a low doleful note, and already as I leant my weight against the tiller I thought with some apprehension of the miles of uneasy seas that lay between us and the shelter of the friendly old Blackwater.

But the sight of Jay's bulky figure crouched in the corner of the cockpit with the dim circle of light from the compass beside him reassured me, and I told myself not to be a chicken. After all, even if I was new to sailing and this short cruise across to Ostend and along to the Scheldt was my very first experience of sailing out of sight of land, Jay was more than twenty years my senior and an experienced cruising man himself and knew what he was doing.

'The old girl's going well, isn't she.' His cheery voice brought warmth to my uneasiness. 'If this wind holds we'll lay it nicely to the Edinburgh. How far? Oh about 75 miles I'd reckon, then into the Barrow Deep and the Swin Spitway, and we'll be home, almost.'

The lights of Vlissingen had long dipped below the horizon astern and the coastal lights towards Zeebrugge looked dim and distant to port, as though they too were ready to be swallowed up in the seas. Here and there the lights of steamers glided past in the eerie and remote manner they have at sea, with no hint of the form of the ship that carried them. But when their single

91

stern light drew away to windward there would be borne down on the night wind that inescapable smell of a steamer, a mixture of coal smoke, hot oil, oily steam, galley odours and the scent of foreign cargoes.

A momentary shuddering from the leech of the mainsail warned me that I was pinching her. We both hardened in the sheets a little and the *Signora* broke into a more lively leaping gait.

'I can't lay better than wNw.' I said at last. 'This wind's heading us.'

It was all too clear now that the wind was not only gaining in strength, but also working more round into the west, which would be almost dead in our teeth. The ebb had run its course and the young flood flowing against the wind was building up the seas so that every now and then you could see their white crests galloping out of the dark. No wonder they were known as white horses.

One of them hit our weather bow with a crash like a gun and we both ducked to avoid the sting of the spray. The old yacht's bow fell into the trough beyond and I felt her shudder from end to end as the bowsprit crashed into the next sea. Her tiller was kicking and took all my strength to hold it.

'That was a nasty one!' Jay's voice chuckled against the howl of the wind. 'I'll take her for a spell. It's past midnight, and maybe you'd like to get something to eat?'

I could only shake my head as I gratefully slumped down into the sheltered corner of the cockpit. Somehow that porridge had become as unsettled as the weather.

A heavier squall boomed out of the night and laid the ship over until the water washed along the lee deck and over the coaming into the cockpit in an alarming cataract of white foam. There was no easing of the wind now; cold, spray-laden and with a shrill mocking cry in the rigging it was coming at us straight out of the wNw. *Signora* lay down and wallowed.

'You all right, Maurice?' Jay peered down at me from the helm. 'Can you haul the stays'l sheet aweather, we've got to get another reef in.' His voice sounded urgent as his hands deftly lashed the tiller to leeward with a quick sliphitch and I swigged in the foresheet. 'That's fine, she'll lie-to quiet enough now. Will you ease the halyards while I bowse down the leech tackle.'

We worked in silence hardly able to see one another in the darkness, but knowing almost by instinct when to ease the throat for the luff cringle, then the peak for Jay to haul down the leech – it was the third and top reef we were putting in – and the tying of the reef points away from the boom. Between us, swaying together like wrestlers on the pitching deck by the mast, we swigged up the peak once more, eased off the topping-lift, and staggered back to the comparative shelter of the cockpit.

'We were a bit out in our weather forecasting, weren't we?' Jay spoke with the chuckle back in his voice, and I noticed that he did not lay any blame at the feet of the Dutch harbour officials. 'We can't run back now,' he added as though he guessed my thoughts, 'we've come too far with this flood tide under us. We'll just have to make the best of it.'

And I suppose make the best of the night was what we did as we let the old yawl drive on a northerly course, close-hauled and with the tide under her lee bow. To me it seemed it was blowing a full gale of wind and the sound of the seas as they raced towards us, their crests glowing white here and there in the darkness, was more than a little unnerving.

Jay lashed the tiller again with the yacht on course and sat down on the floor of the cockpit. 'No need to get cold and wet,' he remarked. 'We're out of the steamer lanes here and the old girl will look after us. Just keep an eye lifting now and again, will you, in case we meet a fisherman from Ostend or the odd coaster.'

In the short time I had been sailing in the Suffolk and Essex rivers I had never encountered a wind like this, nor such steep and high seas, and the experience was proving more frightening than I had imagined possible from the few sailing books I had read. There were then no splendid books like Adlard Coles's *Heavy Weather Sailing*, the Royal Ocean Racing Club had yet to hold its first race round the Fastnet, and few of the yachtsmen one knew had been offshore in a real gale of wind. There were, in fact, few criteria from which to assess what might happen next; and in the blustering darkness amid the wash of angry seas somewhere in the North Sea there seemed to me little comfort and a great deal of threat to our ship.

But as we sat crouched in the cockpit, silent now for there seemed little one could say, I had to admire how well the *Signora* was shouldering her way through the seas and sailing herself close-hauled towards the North. She had been built in about 1890 with the straight stem, counter stern and long straight keel of the period, rather narrow and deep, and she seemed entirely at home in these elements as though she was willing to nurse her two tired occupants and take them back to more sheltered waters. Certainly it was a relief to be able to shelter out of the wind and stinging spray in the deep cockpit, for it is prolonged exposure to cold conditions and the resulting fatigue that demoralizes a yacht's crew and causes them to make mistakes or to give up altogether.

Not long ago I was reading a book in which the author described some of the races and cruises he had made in a newly-built sloop of about 26 ft overall length. The boat was of a modern type designed by a leading yacht designer, and had already proved how successful and fast she was by winning more than one challenge cup in handicap racing, a really first-class design of her contemporary type.

While returning from a holiday cruise on the Continent with the owner and two others aboard she encountered fresh to strong winds in the North Sea. She showed how competently she could shoulder her way over them and keep going at a high speed more or less close-hauled through these unpleasant conditions. But a point the author made was that because she was so quick on the helm somebody had to helm the boat, as he put it, every mile of the way. For not even one minute could the helm be left and the boat relied upon to look after herself and stay on her course. Steering became so cold and wet and tiring that as the hours went by the owner and his young crew could stand only short spells at the tiller, and in due time they all began to suffer from exposure and fatigue.

In the event they stuck it out, nothing fortunately parted or gave way (for she was a well-built and fully-equipped modern yacht) and they made their harbour on this side safely in due course. But it is under such conditions of crew strain and exhaustion that wrong decisions can be made and accidents can happen.

You cannot, however, expect to find everything in any one boat. On a normal beat to windward, for instance, this little modern sloop would probably have sailed rings round an old timer like the *Signora*. Her quickness on the helm would score many times in any race over the old yawl's leisurely manner in staying, and those are qualities that win races. But in strong winds and bad weather off shore the ancient straight stemmer would lie-to with staysail aback and helm to leeward, or ease herself over the seas close-hauled with helm lashed for hours on end, permitting her crew to relax and rest and avoid long exposure to the wet and the cold.

Today's highly-developed cruiser-racing sloops with their light displacement, short fin-keels and spade rudders are wonderful machines for fast sailing, and over and over again they have proved their success as a type in off-shore racing with a strong and competent crew, but on any long passage cruise in hard conditions these yachts are tough on those who sail them.

When the sky first began to pale in the east and we could make out the grey-and-white flecked outlines of the seas I was appalled at their steepness and the way they reared above us as we crouched in the cockpit. But the game little yawl continued to stagger her way over and through them, heeled to her covering board close-reefed, her taut burgee already ragged at the masthead after the night's blow.

Jay's face looked hollow and grey with cold, as though he had suddenly aged twenty years. He noticed my glance and broke into a welcome smile.

'It's all right, Maurice,' he said huskily. 'I've taken my teeth out so I can't lose 'em!'

The flood tide was almost done and soon the ebb would be running away towards the North. 'We'll go about now,' Jay said, 'and get the ebb under our lee bow. Can you help me with the foresheets?'

Signora came up slowly into the wind, lifted her bows over a breaking crest, then fell into the trough crashing her long bowsprit into the next sea. She stopped dead, all life gone out of her, and before we could get the staysail aback her head fell off

95

again on to the port tack. Once more we looked for a smooth amidst the welter of grey-and-white water, and once again she missed stays. But the third time we were lucky and soon the yawl was heeled over and lunging ahead on the starboard tack, heading a little south of west.

Perhaps to take our minds off the wet and uncomfortable conditions, or for something to talk about, my skipper explained what underbowing the tide meant and why it was important. When you have to tack across the main run of the tides, he said, as when crossing the North Sea or the Channel, it always pays to sail on the tack which keeps the tide pressing against your lee bow. Provided you have plenty of sea room you should keep on that tack until the tide turns, and then go about on to the other tack. With the tide pressing against your lee bow your ship is helped to windward, whereas if you sail with the tide on your weather bow you are not only carried bodily to leeward, but your additional speed to leeward brings the *apparent* wind, the direction of wind your burgee shows, more ahead, and you lose even more ground to leeward. It was a lesson learnt in hard circumstances that I have never forgotten.

Looking back over the years at this my first experience of a gale in a little yacht at sea, it seems very small beer in the telling. Many of today's yachtsmen put on a show of indifference to gales: 'Pooh, just a capful of wind,' they would say, 'nothing to make a song about.' Perhaps they are right, but when we lose the ability to pause and wonder at some of nature's phenomena we must lose some of our sense of proportion, for however lovely it may be on a fine day the sea is a pitiless monster in repose and the sea winds are giants in their strength.

But in recent years hundreds of yachts have made long ocean voyages and ridden out countless gales, a few have encountered a hurricane and survived, the annual trek across the Atlantic to the West Indies has become a family migration, and circum-navigating the world by way of the Horn may soon become a yachtsman's status symbol. But it is as well to bear in mind that every year, through boating articles in the press or a visit to the Boat Show in London newcomers venture into the world of small boats with little learning and no experience, buy a small yacht, sally forth as the books advise, and meet their first capful of wind. Like one's first day at school or first air raid, it is always a frightening and moving experience.

So it was to me in my greenness as I retched over the lee coaming and wished the poor old *Signora* would stand still a moment or sink.

'The dinghy's gone. Look at this.' Jay showed me the frayed end of the little boat's painter. 'Anyway, it's been swamped for the past hour or two, so it won't be such a drag on the old girl.' I had to admire his philosophical attitude.

The sky in the east was already lighter and I realized I must have been dozing for two hours or more in the corner of the cockpit, for I was stiff and cold and could not stop shivering. Now we could see the seas to windward and follow the white tracery work down their backs as they raced away to leeward I was appalled at their height but impressed at the same time at our little yawl's ability to take each one on her chin and sidle over it with only spray to drench her.

A steamer of an older type, a deep-laden three-island tramp with the smoke blowing astern from her tall black funnel, crossed our bows half a mile distant and bound no doubt for London's river. She looked a fine sight as her bluff bows plunged rhythmically and reared skyward while the spray blew aft over her bridge in white puffs like steam. From her rusty decks I imagined the little *Signora* must have looked like a mid-Victorian engraving entitled 'Yacht Racing in a Storm'.

'Not much sense getting too perished with cold.' The wind almost whipped the words out of the skipper's mouth. 'Could you face a mug of tea – a bite of breakfast perhaps?'

I took the hint and forced myself below to the galley. Somehow with the coming of day I felt less seasick, and by the time I had made a good pot of tea and produced some boiled eggs and bread and butter we were both able to crouch on the floor of the deep cockpit and eat. Immediately we felt like new and stronger men.

When the flood tide had done and the north-going ebb had set in we put the ship about on to the starboard tack again to keep the tide pressing against our lee bow. Again she would not have it the first time, and we had to make three attempts and once more watch carefully for a comparative smooth in the seas, before I was able to get the staysail aback and slew her head round. Staying these old straight-stem yachts in broken water was always a mixture of art and luck and hard work on the sheets.

As the long day wore on and the sun appeared from out of the clouds and neared the western horizon, there seemed a little lessening in the strength of the wind. The whole sea no longer looked like a heaving white carpet, but those steep ones that rose between us and the sun were shot through their translucent depths with exquisite greens and blues, so lovely that one gasped at the sight.

Towards dark we picked up the red flash of the Gunfleet pile lighthouse, and already the seas were becoming smaller and less vicious as we began to feel the lee of the sands. We had found our way into the northern end of the East Swin without sighting either the Longsand Head or the Sunk Head buoys.

'It's coming up to high water,' said my skipper. 'When the ebb sets in it would be useless trying to bash our way into Harwich, as that would be out of our course, anyway. We'll let go under the lee of these sands and have a few hours' sleep until the next flood starts.'

I reflected what a wise old bird the skipper was: another yachtsman would probably have carried on for the rest of the night trying to work up against the tide to reach Harwich, merely to be in harbour. With old Jay's knowledge of this coast we took bearings of the Gunfleet light on our starboard beam and sounded in towards the sands until the leadsman called, 'By the mark, three!'

Here with old Cold Nose down and her sails stowed and riding light on the forestay, *Signora* lay snug enough under the lee of the Gunfleet, lifting and falling to seas that rapidly became less and less as the ebb flowed away north and the sands to windward started to uncover. And below in the soft lamp-light in the cabin, what relief to rinse our salt-encrusted faces in fresh water, have a quick meal, and then roll into our blankets for five hours' blessed rest!

It was daylight and the yacht rolling beam on with the young flood running when we turned out and got her under way

98

again. The wind was still wNw. but easing, and we carried whole mainsail, staysail and No. 2 jib as we beat up Swin and sounded our way gingerly through the Swin-Wallet Spitway in just over one fathom.

Later in the day, near high water, the old *Signora* luffed up into the entrance to Heybridge Basin and the scent of hay and flowers in bloom from across the fields was soft and warm after the cold tang of the sea. As she sidled gently against the quay-side and the lock keeper took our lines, he remarked, 'So you come across from the other side last night? Must've had a dustin', didn't you?'

'We've had *two* nights of it', my skipper replied with modesty. 'It was a rather bumpy trip. Had to hold our hats on all the way.'

That, I thought, summed it up neatly, but I secretly felt that it had been an experience I should always be glad to have had.

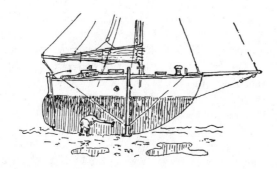

Wilful, 8 tons

9. *Pilot cutter and Irish jaunt*

THAT cruise across the North Sea was the last sail I had in the *Signora*, for the skipper's job caused him to move his home down to the West Country. Like me, he tended to change his boats every so often, although not perhaps so frequently as I did or for quite so many irrational reasons and I was not surprised to learn soon after that he had replaced the old yawl with another elderly boat, a West-Country cutter like a Falmouth quay punt but without the leg-o'-mutton mizzen or dandy.

Meanwhile after two years' hard work in London with little sailing and no boat of my own I felt the call of the sea more urgently than ever, and with what promised to be steady and reasonably paid employment I started to look round again for a small boat. Through the agency department of our lamented fortnightly I was able to study details of boats for sale in the under £100 category, and there seemed to be quite a number of them. But after spending more than enough in rail fares and travelling down by crowded Saturday trains to such places as Erith, Grays, Leigh-on-Sea, Fambridge and even to Maldon, I was reduced to thinking that there was nothing riverworthy (let alone seaworthy) amongst such a collection of junky tore-outs and decaying old cutters.

Finally one day in the saltings at Burnham-on-Crouch I came across an old-time black cutter whose appearance took my fancy. She was a 6-tonner with a smart clipper bow, a neat round counter stern, a lofty pole mast and an attractive sheer-line. Her name was *Puffin* II, and I learnt that she was about 31 ft in length, 7 ft 8 in. beam, 4 ft 8 in. draught, and had been built at Bideford in North Devon back in 1897, the year of *Swan*. After coming to terms with her owner and surveying her against the quay the following weekend I bought her.

My friend Jay had sold me *Signora*'s mooring off the Black-water Sailing Clubhouse at Heybridge, as he would no longer need it, but before taking *Puffin* round to her new home port I kept her for a few weeks on a mooring near the Royal Corinthian where the charge, including looking after the boat during the week, was then only six shillings weekly. There was always plenty to see at Burnham and at that time there were still numbers of big yachts with paid hands, to admire. Mr Tredwen's barge *Pearl* was also there, and I sometimes saw the old man himself, with his white hair and kindly ruddy face, joining her from the Corinthian hard on a Saturday afternoon. He used to get down to the Corinthian most weekends in summer and winter alike, and kept the *Pearl* in commission all the year round.

One day the yard boatman came alongside *Puffin* for a yarn, and pointed out a big yawl across the fairway. 'See that deck-'ouse, sir?' he said. 'They give her that last year. You see the mainboom just about clears the top of it by not more'n a few inches. Well, sir, one day it was a flat calm and they'd set the mainsail and was waitin' for a breeze so they could let goo the the moorin'. One of the gen'lemen what come down with the owner, a guest it was with eyeglass, yottin' cap an' all, was standin' leanin' his elbows on the top of that 'ere deck'ouse lookin' at nothin' in partic'lar acrorst the water with his back to the mains'l which was just over the rail. And then that 'ere mainboom – it's a tidy weight, I can tell you, sir – began to swing inboard ever so slow and gentlelike. It come nearly amidships and just nudged the back of the gen'leman's head and nipped him between it and the deck'ouse. The gen'leman opened his mouth to let out a holler, but didn't make no sound – I could see it all as plain as I see you now, sir – and then the boom just as gentlelike and slow swung outboard again, and when the gen'leman stood up there was his false teeth buried in the deck'ouse. You can see the marks there now, sir, if you was to row acrorst and goo aboard.'

Puffin had a small engine with a built-in reluctance to start, or if once started to keep going for more than half an hour or so. It was a single-cylinder two-stroke 3-horsepower of ancient lineage, not unlike a small brother, with many of the more undesirable family failings of *Signora*'s thunderous monster. This three-ponypower piece of ironmongery did not use the more

101

modern petroil fuel mixture, but like its big brother ran on neat petrol which was infused with drops of oil at regular intervals from a charming little steam-engine-type sight-feed lubricator with a glass tube which was bolted to the side of the cylinder. Regularly this lubricator became unscrewed by the engine's violent vibration and dropped into the bilge, and after a time the engine, missing its greasy appendage, duly came to a turgid stop. Like many others of its kind, this two-stroke was noisy, it stank, and it had all those other hateful habits that I came to associate with similar installations; but it was part of *Puffin* and as it gave her a dizzy speed of three knots in calm water I used it when I was obliged to do so.

Puffin proved a delight to sail, for although her tiller was very short and the rudder fairly large she was so well balanced that you could steer her with two fingers most of the time. Punching into the short seas of the Whittaker Channel and the Wallet on a weather-going tide she was dry, for the flare in the fiddlehead bow threw the spray away to port and starboard, but she showed herself to be an adept at pile-driving. That is to say, she plunged her bow into each sea as if she loved it and wanted to embrace them all, and when her bows rose over a steep one her flat counter would give the water a sharp smack as though to say, 'There, take *that*, for making such a fuss of my front end!' She really was a tosser and pitcher with her lofty mast and hollow run, and once when anchored in a short swell at the mouth of the Crouch she kept on dipping her foredeck under and sending shakes down the anchor cable that hit the river bed with dull thuds. But even though she, poor little dear, was only a stopgap and all I could find for my money that year, it was great to have one's own boat again and to be able to get down by train for a weekend of sea winds away from the pall of London.

Most yachtsmen still travelled down to their boats by train, for the explosion in private motoring and a car for every family was only about to begin. Weekend return tickets available from Friday midday until Monday were issued at a cut rate of a single fare plus one third, and a weekend return third class from Liverpool Street to Burnham cost as little as 6*s* 6*d*. Another useful facility was the yachtsman's weekend ticket which permitted one to use the return half from a different port from that booked, so that you could sail round the coast and come back on the same ticket, paying only for excess mileage if the return station was farther from Liverpool Street. These tickets on the London and North Eeastern were a legacy of Great Eastern Railway days and had been introduced, I believe, through the efforts made by the Cruising Association, an active body founded in 1908 by a group of Corinthian yachtsmen sharing a keen love of coastal sailing in small craft.

Relying on trains and buses and with no parked car to tie one down, I made full use of these tickets that summer, and with friends or alone sailed *Puffin* up and down the East Coast, returning Sunday evening or very early Monday morning from places as far apart as Maldon, Wivenhoe, Pin Mill and Ipswich, Woodbridge or even Aldeburgh. It was carefree cruising and essentially simple, for with only bus and rail timetables to study we travelled light with rucksacks on our backs, prepared to walk from Hard to station, or even the two miles from the Maldon terminus to the moorings at Heybridge. Bread, sausages, meat, bacon, eggs, tinned milk, all the basic food for a weekend you bought at the local stores which purposely kept open late on a Friday night. You were then free to take a fair wind round to any other part of the coast that beckoned, and catch the London train on Sunday evening from whatever anchorage you reached.

It was only when everyone began to arrive by car, and wives and family appeared aboard nearly every yacht, that weekend sailing changed into a burdensome expedition. The hards on Saturday mornings became crowded with quaintly garbed men, women and children, accompanied by mountains of food baskets, clothes, rolls of bedding and pillows, clean towels and kitchen cloths, detergents and toys and teddy bears and bottles of Daddy's lifesaver, perhaps a dog or two – all the weekend family paraphernalia to be piled into a protesting dinghy with a shiny popping outboard on the stern. But more yachts were beginning to give pleasure to far more people, children's squeaky voices mingled happily with the skipper's shouted orders, and a sail to the mouth of the river and back to the moorings, and so home again by the car, became the normal routine. The happy-go-lucky days of round-the-coast cruising whether the weather

103

was good or bad were on the way out. The latest and most important of the household gods was taking possession and holding the little ship closely to her home mooring: it was the family car.

In London I met a quiet slender girl with dark shingled hair who was writing articles for the yachting papers under her pen name Peter Gerard. Her love of the sea was patent, for she had read avidly such writers as C. Fox Smith, Basil Lubbock, Keble Chatterton, Villiers and others, and knew more about the voyages of the square riggers than I ever did, and she nursed a passion for rough coasters and fishing craft and sturdy sea-going yachts like the quay punts of Falmouth. Peter was no dinghy dolly ready to crew some helmsman in Saturday races round the buoys: she hated such stuff and told me what she longed for was a real ship she could command and call her own. To see her in her London clothes you would not guess how wiry and tough and utterly fearless she could be when once afloat.

Once or twice when I was too engrossed with the printers near press day to leave London for the weekend, I lent her *Puffin*, and this strange girl sailed the little clipper round the coast from Heybridge to Pin Mill and back on her own. 'She's a fine little ship,' she said, 'but if she were mine I'd turf that smelly, useless engine overboard! A handy boat like *Puffin* doesn't need an engine.' It seemed inevitable, therefore, that we should get married and share the little ship cruising together, and her insistence that it would be far more seamanlike and less costly than a flat in London if we were to live on board a boat somewhere on the coast seemed a reasonable idea at first. Peter would continue to write her articles aboard while keeping the ship homely and ready for getting underway at weekends, while I should commute daily by train to London.

Puffin was obviously too small and cramped for living aboard, and she was accordingly sold. The search began for a comfortable old vessel roomy enough to take our books and homely possessions but not too heavy for us to manage together, and a few weeks before the day of the wedding we were led to *Afrin*, a 10-tonner, which like my *Puffin* was found lying in the saltings just above Burnham. Once on board her roomy decks and inside the richly teak-panelled saloon we knew she was to be our homely ship. *Afrin*, we learned, had been built at Lowestoft in 1883 as a local pilot cutter, and we noticed that her round counter stern had the planks of the deep taffrail laid vertically in traditional pilot-boat fashion. She measured 34 ft overall, 10 ft beam, and drew about 3 ft forward and 4 ft 3 in. aft; her midsection was just like a small coaster's and this width below the waterline accounted for the very wide cabin floor and ample lockers. The after end of the coachroof was extended some 18 in. over the deep cockpit and here, under a box forming a sheltered seat, crouched a rusty piece of machinery that at once warmed my heart. It was a two-cylinder Kelvin which not only looked but we later ascertained was a model of 1908 vintage. For squatting upright on the mud by a jetty within reach of the station during the week, and for exploring the rivers and creeks of the Thames Estuary at weekends, the old *Afrin* seemed ideal: the mate approved of her, and she became ours.

After the wedding at one of Wren's lovely old churches in the City my wife and I joined the old cutter at Burnham for our honeymoon of ten days – all we could take off at the time. Our plans to sail across to Holland were, probably just as well, frustrated by light easterly airs, and we sailed instead into the familiar anchorages between the Blackwater and the Alde. *Afrin*'s conversion into a yacht had been completed by a house builder in Ipswich named Fisk who had put into her all the attractive teak panelling in the cabin and the unusual carved arch doorway into the fo'c'sle. Her interior had a warm and homely atmosphere which was helped by the coal fire that burned merrily on cold and wet days. The tiller was an oft coveted feature, of teak 6 ft long and carved in rope patterns with a 9 in. brass ferrule at the hand end round which the tiller lines worked smoothly.

Yet despite this powerful tiller we were at first dismayed to find that *Afrin* griped so much in any breeze, slewing into the wind like a weathercock against the helmsman's sweating efforts, that we began to hate her. 'You're nothing but a hard-mouthed old cow!' the mate spat at her as she stood in her seaboots, slacks, grey jersey and wool cap hauling at the tiller tackle; and her expression would have cowed a more delicate boat. If the staysail was lowered and we tried to sail under

105

working jib and mainsail only the old ship refused to pay off in stays unless we let run the mainsheet. That kind of treatment did not make for smart windward work in the river, and on one occasion beating down through the crowded anchorage at Burnham on a fast-running ebb we missed stays and all but got ourselves athwart another yacht's bows. 'She's a bitch!' cried the mate and I echoed her opinion sadly.

Iron ballast in firebars and pigs was stowed under the fo'c'sle floor as well as packed tightly up to the floorboards in the cabin, and at anchor later that day we set to and shifted all the ballast from the fo'c'sle and stowed it abaft the engine. *Afrin* now floated 2 in. higher at the bow and some 3 in. down at the stern, and when we rowed round her we were pleased to note how much better and more upstanding she looked: she looked more handsome and her trim suited her. Next day when we got underway we could scarcely believe she was the same boat. Under main and working jib she was as handy as could be, went about without hesitation and payed off to leeward even with the mainsheet closehauled. Peter's weatherbeaten face wore a kindlier expression. 'We've tamed her,' was all she said, and I knew we were going to love the old cutter once more.

By trial and error, I remembered, *Storm*'s tendency to gripe hard in strong winds had been cured by shifting ballast aft, to give the forefoot less grip of the water and the stern more, and *Afrin* was again showing us how important it is to trim a yacht correctly, especially one of the old kind with long straight keel, in order to get the best out of her. Most yachts built today have all the weight cast in their keels and no inside ballast which can be moved to adjust the vessels' trim. It is in many cases a retrograde step, for I have known more than one widely advertised and costly product which has proved abominable to steer on any course in breezy weather, and cried out to be properly trimmed. Some inside trimming ballast is useful, too, in a cruising yacht, for lightening or careening her to reduce her draught if she has had the misfortune to go aground at the top of high water with the tides daily taking off, and is in danger of being neaped for the next ten days or more.

For the remainder of that season *Afrin* found a convenient berth by the yacht-club jetty at Walton-on-Naze, from where I could catch the early-morning train to London and return to the ship by 2000 hrs. It meant five long and exhausting days during the week, but we were both young, and still enjoyed getting underway and sailing hard over the weekend. And some of it was hard sailing, for that summer of 1927 was one of the wettest and consistently windiest on record, and from my log-book I see that for six consecutive weekends there were two reefs in our mainsail which we had not shaken out.

I had another ten days of summer holiday due to come, for our jobs made it impossible for either of us to get away for more than a week or ten days at a time, and a letter had come from a charming correspondent in County Limerick telling me that he had entered his 20 ton brigantine for this year's Fastnet Race, and would Peter and I care to sign on as he was expecting his sister Kate to be one of the crew. It was Conor O'Brien and his interesting ship was the 42 ft *Saoirse* (Erse for freedom and pro-nounced 'seershay') in which he had already sailed round the world by way of Cape Horn. She had a poop deck with waist-high taffrail and was rigged for deep-water voyaging with square course and topsail on the mainmast, a gunter lug on the mizzen, a staysail between the masts, and inner and outer jibs on a steeved bowsprit. It was a heaven-sent opportunity to sail with a celebrated circumnavigator (O'Brien told the story of this and other voyages in his *Across Three Oceans*) and to try square rig.

With her high bluff bows, long-steeved bowsprit with safety netting beneath, low waist amidships with 2 ft-high bulwarks, the low square deckhouse over the poopdeck aft and her black-and-grey hull, *Saoirse* when we joined her at Cowes looked strikingly like one of the smaller Irish coasters. Conor O'Brien, short, stocky, red-haired and with merry blue eyes in a tanned elfin face, was full of fire and Irish jocularity and raring to get his ship to sea and away from all this land. His sister Kate was quiet, but proved to be a stalwart and reliable hand and happily she and Peter took to one another on sight. The rest of the crew, like me, had just joined and were new to the ship and her complicated gear.

This was to be the third Fastnet race. The first race had been held two years before in 1925, when in the face of uninformed press criticism seven yachts took part. The next year there were nine competitors and the Ocean Racing Club (soon to be made Royal) was formed. This time 15 yachts, including our oddly manned Irish brigantine, started from Cowes in unpleasant misty weather with a falling glass and a rising south-west wind on the 615-mile course eastabout the Isle of Wight to the Fastnet rock off the sw. corner of Eire and home to Plymouth. As *Saoirse* rolled and lurched in the gathering seas past the Bembridge Ledge buoy and out into the gloom of the Channel the double note of the Nab Tower foghorn followed us, plaintive and thin through the driving rain, and I can even now clearly hear the doleful two tones *whee-whaw* above the wash of the seas and the occasional shudder from aloft as the square topsail luff shook in the wind.

Compared with today's great fleets of small yachts that take part in the biennial Fastnet event, all of them as taut-rigged as a metre-class boat, their decks littered with shiny mechanical aids and the man at the wheel faced with a consol full of dials, it is interesting to pause and recollect what sort of yachts those fifteen were that lifted and plunged into the Channel gale that August of 1927.

One entry had sailed over from New York, the Alden-designed 58 ft schooner *Nicanor*, and a near sister ship from the same designer's board but built in England and only just launched, was the 54 ft schooner *La Goleta*, 29 tons T.M. The celebrated ex-French pilot cutter *Jolie Brise* 44 tons T.M.; *Ilex* 20 ton yawl; *Altair* 14 ton cutter; and *Penboch* French-built 12 ton cutter had all taken part in the previous year's race. The newcomers included *Tally Ho*, Albert Strange-designed 29 ton cutter; *Morwenna*, Linton Hope-designed schooner 28 tons; *Spica*, 22 ton cutter; *Shira* 21 ton cutter; *Content* 19 ton cutter; *Thalassa* 16 ton yawl; *Maitenes* 12 ton cutter; and the ex-Colchester smack *Nellie* 12 ton cutter. There was not a racing type amongst them, and gaff rig predominated.

As darkness closed in the weather deteriorated and on board *Saoirse* first the staysail and the square topsail had to be sent down, then the inner jib handed and the gunter mizzen reefed. Those of us who were green hands aboard this strange ship bucking like a bronco became sick in turn, but we all managed

108

to keep on our feet to learn as fast as possible where the many ropes were belayed and what they were attached to. In the screaming darkness and driving spray and wild motion it was not the easiest schooling, but watches were set and in time shadowy figures in black oilskins on deck became recognizable. *Saoirse*'s short and bluff hull climbed the great Channel seas and seemed to fall bodily over their crests while her long bowsprit alternatively stabbed the sky and the face of the next oncoming comber.

Only very slowly were we working to windward under the reduced canvas against this wind which was officially logged Force 8. The skies cleared during the second day and when the sun came out the scene all round us was majestic and beautiful in the extreme: great moving hills of translucent green with white tracery-flecked backs racing away to leeward when we had climbed up and over them. Weak from sickness and lack of proper sleep we stood our watches, hazily trying to remember whether it was dark or daylight during our last watch, and tending to imagine that we were steering the game little ship over hilly grassland that seemed perpetually on the move. And still the wind held in the south-west and blew and blew.

Thirteen of the fifteen starters gave up and put back into port. The two stalwarts that held on and doggedly fought out the race between them were the narrow and deep transom-sterned flush-decked gaff cutter *Tally Ho* and the brand-new handsome gaff schooner *La Goleta*, which was declared the winner. These two yachts set a tradition for keeping in the race whatever the weather that helped to make the R.O.R.C. events the enormous success they eventually became.

With her waist periodically full of water up to the bulwarks *Saoirse* in two days, the skipper reckoned, was just about abreast Portland Bill when we imagined the rest of the fleet were probably stretched out beyond Start Point or even the Lizard. 'Sure, I nivver did mean to sail to wind'ard,' exclaimed Conor as his blue eyes swept the windy sky. 'We'll go the way she likes it best!' And with wheel up and a vastly kinder motion we ran back to the Needles and the Solent in ten hours, a distance we had taken two days to fight for, aware now of the great qualities of this tough little vessel which had run her way round the world.

And with Conor's light-hearted Irish banter and a general easing of tension it was one of the happiest and fastest sails – for we soon had the square topsail set over the main – I think we landlubbers ever had. And when it came to parting from our winsome skipper and his ship my wife's day was made when he exclaimed 'You've all been a good crew, but I'll tell you that Peter's been the best hand I've ever had!' No wonder that in the train coming home she was heard to muse 'One day, sonny boy, *we'll* have a little ship and sail round the world, *and* she'll be square rigged.'

Dear Conor, he was one of the most provocative and delightful of correspondents and I always enjoyed publishing his articles on deep-sea cruising and yachts' gear. His training as an architect gave him a great ability to put his often original ideas about rigging and yachts' ironwork clearly in drawings, and his book *Deep-Water Yacht Rig* (O.U.P.) although outdated by today's offshore yachts, is something of a classic. The *Yachting Monthly* and cruising fraternity sustained a sad loss when he passed on.

At the end of the season Peter said, 'I shall never rest until I have a ship of my very own, to be my own skipper and sail her how and where I like.' No compromise we discussed appeared to be feasible, and when we moved into a flat in London that autumn our old *Afrin* was sold. She was bought by a man and his wife who decided to explore the East Coast before sailing her round to the Solent, but the second time they took her out from Harwich they hit the remains of H.M.S. *Arethusa*, sunk on the Cutler shoal off Bawdsey in 1916, and our old home went down swiftly with her sails still set and drawing. My main regret on hearing the news was that I could not have salvaged her handsome tiller to hang on my office wall. I should like it now as a reminder of a bygone age.

With her share of the proceeds of the sale of *Afrin* Peter went off looking for her dream ship, and found her in the shape of a 30-year-old Falmouth-built yawl, like a quay punt but with a counter stern. She was a handsome 7-tonner, 32 ft overall with nearly 6 ft draught and with no engine. She needed a complete refit, and Peter worked on her every day scraping and painting, happy at last with her own command. It began a partnership

110

that was to last unbroken for over 40 years, an example of faithfulness to one ship that with my temperament I could never hope to emulate.

The glimpse of deep-water sailing that *Saoirse* had given us awakened in me a desire to sail farther off shore than the coast and creeks which had been my home ground of contentment for so long, and as Peter seemed well content with her yawl I decided to try a real deep-sea type. As a complete change from any of my previous experiments I bought *Wilful,* an 8 ton gaff cutter with a flush deck, transom stern, and a small zinc-lined cockpit right aft. She measured 30 ft overall with 8 ft 6 in. beam and drew something over 5 ft 6 in. with a heavy lead keel, and had been built in 1899 by Sibbick of Cowes. Between the dark-mahogany panelled saloon with its tiled and brass fireplace and the cockpit there had been a small two-berth cabin – the ladies' cabin, reminiscent of many old-time yachts – but this had been turned into an engine-room for the bulky twin-cylinder paraffin Kelvin.

Just what I hoped to achieve with a deep draught boat of this rugged type, tied as I was five days a week to a desk in London, I cannot now recall. But we based both yachts in the Twizzle at Walton, and most weekends when I could escape from press work we sailed in company. Not unexpectedly with their similar deep draught, in the Pye Channel and other shoal places the two boats sometimes went on the putty together! Sailing in company is always good for one's seamanship and endeavours to get the best out of one's own boat, and apart from racing it is the best way to find out the relative behaviour of different yachts. For example, we found that when beating into a short head sea *Wilful* with her lean bow would slice through the seas and gain steadily on the yawl, which had a somewhat fuller bow with a pronounced flare and full deckline. But off the wind or on a broad reach there was little to choose between the two in getting over the ground.

Peter was always a pioneer. At a time when few women wore slacks she gave up wearing a skirt even on shore and had trouser suits made for her thirty years before they became fashionable. She had a neat shelter built over the fore end of her boat's cock-pit which gave her fine protection when thrashing to windward,

111

long before doghouses or any kind of windbreak became fashionable in small yachts. And to help pay for her ship's upkeep she also started a school afloat for teaching young women sailing and seamanship. She received so many applications that for most weeks throughout the summer she was away cruising in the old yawl with one or two girl cadets aboard. The training was thorough and more than one cadet booked another week's course for the following year. Under the watchful eye of their fearless skipper the more experienced girls, in age ranging from perhaps 20 to 40-odd, were taken on coasting cruises across the Thames Estuary, to Ostend, or some way down Channel. Peter and her much-loved ship had found their vocation.

As the *Yachting Monthly* slowly pulled itself out of the previous years of doldrums and began to make a profit again, work steadily increased, for in our London flat I was not only taking on extra press work but had started to design small cruising yachts as well. The first had been a very shallow-draught centreboarder of 8 tons named *Wind Song*, designed for a client who asked for a boat for wild fowling in winter, and she had been built at Portsmouth in 1928. Further commissions necessitated working at the drawing board through weekends while Peter was away on her seamanship courses. *Wilful* was now on the Hamble, where we had sailed her during a part of our summer holiday, and as I was finding less and less time to use a boat of that deep-draught type, I sold her there. Her buyer was a yachtsman of experience from Lymington who was to own and cherish her for many years and to become one of my oldest friends.

My regret at parting with the Sibbick cutter was tempered a little by the realization that her wild seesaw pitching motion in a head sea, which I learnt could be attributed to heavy displacement coupled to fine ends and a deep keel acting like a pendulum was more than I could bear at sea. Whereas *Saoirse* had had us all sick because we were punching into a full gale in the Channel, *Wilful* was the only yacht I have ever owned that could make me seasick when diving to windward through even a modest chop. It was as though she knew I never really liked boats with very deep draught, whatever their size, and whenever her lean bows dropped into a trough *Wilful* gave me

5. *Lone Gull 1*, 10-ton centreboard cutter, built 1938

6. Sir Frederick Browning's *Jeanne d'Arc* was an experiment in wishbone rig

upward kicks at the helm like a horse – which played merry hell with one's inside.

Splendid little cruiser though she was, with such a fine record, I felt her contempt for a ditch-crawler owner who loved all the shallow places and preferred an Essex smack to the slimmest and fastest Solent yacht, and she had a skittish way of showing it. Poor *Wilful*, admired by so many, was another of my mistakes.

10. *Interlude for smacks*

As the smack roared past Holliwell Point and turned her long bowsprit down the Crouch the whole surface of the river looked like a carpet of little white horses. The flood was running up against a strong wind from a little south of west. From the tracery of foam on the surface we reckoned it was blowing more than force 6 and logged it as a steady seven. And it was cold, too, perishing cold, because it was in the middle of January and there was sleet in the air.

Frank Shuttlewood had been right when we arrived at his yard at Paglesham to fetch her round to Heybridge and he said in his singsong Essex accent, 'You'll want all your reefs in that mains'l today, Mr Griffiths.' He should know, standing there a stocky figure in jersey and kneeboots beside the big black shed, for in that shed his grandfather and then his father had built oyster smacks, barges and small barge yachts, and he knew as well as anyone on the river how to handle a smack.

My old colleague from the office, Norman Clackson, was steering. Norman, six foot five and broad shouldered, looked like a great Viking in his black thighboots and oilskins as he balanced himself with feet well apart on the deck leaning against the tiller. Peter, muffled to the eyes, was standing in the after cabin, only her head and shoulders above the hatchway.

'We're running by the lee, old son,' said Norman. 'We'd better gybe.'

Although the mainsail was close-reefed it was more than I could manage to overhaul the sheet smartly enough, and Norman had to give me a hand to haul in and check the shock of the gybe.

'Guess you've bitten off more than you can chew this time,' said Peter, and I began to think she might be right.

For long enough after *Storm* I had wanted to own a real

smack, and this was it. We had found her on the River Roach, a typical smack built at Brightlingsea no one knew when, some 34 ft overall, 10 ft 3 in. beam, drawing 3 ft forward and 4 ft 6 in. aft, with the low freeboard, 12 in. high bulwarks and wide square counter of the normal Colchester oyster smack. There was no cockpit, only a hatch beneath the tiller to the stern locker or lazarette, but a coachroof gave near-standing headroom in the two-berth after cabin and the saloon, and there was a bogie stove burning brightly and keeping up a comforting warmth below. Once again I had acquired a ship with no engine. Her name had been *Evadne*, but we could not tolerate that one and after our old love we renamed her *Afrina*.

This was not the sort of day or time of year to choose for even a short hop round the land, but Norman's time like mine was limited to weekends and he had volunteered to help us this weekend to get *Afrina* round to Heybridge Basin, where she could lie alongside my wife's yawl while fitting-out. It would be a proper test of the smack's gear, we said, while with this wind about wsw we should be under the lee of the land most of the way. And if any of the gear did carry away we reckoned that with this spring flood running to windward to hold us up we should be able to make the Colne and some shelter under a headsail, the forestays'l perhaps, if the need arose. It is commonplace seamanship in strong weather or when relying on an engine to plan an escape route should anything go wrong aloft or the engine fail suddenly.

Through the Rays'n the surface of the water was a mild turmoil and continually slopped aboard over the weather rail, but there was no real sea, for the Dengie Flats lay just to windward of us. Once round the Bachelor Spit, however, when we came on the wind and hardened in the sheets there were breaking seas with the weather-going tide in the Blackwater, and *Afrina* began to push her lean bow right through them, her foredeck buried under a welter of foam, while the water rushed aft and sloshed round our seaboots. The tiller was pulling hard, too, and we had to lean our weight against it with feet braced against the lee rail. It was already evident that she was yet another boat that was ballasted too much by the head.

115

Our office-softened hands were already raw from wrestling with the stiff sheets, and we decided we could not face the nine-mile beat to windward up to Heybridge in weather like this, although we felt the smack would be game enough and even enjoy it. We accordingly dropped our hook in Mersea Quarters for the night, warming our numbed hands and feet round the cabin fire. And next morning the wind had blown itself out, and with only a light south-west breeze we had the satisfaction of working our ship under sail up the cables length of narrow gut leading to the Basin. Like the great weight she was, the smack carried her way nicely into the lock as the sails were stowed and the lockmaster caught our lines.

This little manoeuvre going into or out of Heybridge lock under sail alone was usually a matter of principle amongst the yachts based in the Basin whenever the wind was suitable. The barges, of course, having no engines, always had to rely on their sails, quant or warps when they brought in loads of split wood from the Baltic steamers which brought up lower down in the deep water below Osea Island. On one occasion, however, something went wrong.

A heavily laden barge was creeping in towards the gut, her fores'l dropped, mains'l brailed up, and only the tops'l aloft to catch the light airs coming over the river wall. The usual group of tidetime spectators stood around the lock watching her slowly come in. Suddenly out of the blue sky a sharp squall filled the tops'l. Before the barge hand at the skipper's holler had time to jump to the tops'l halyards she had begun to forge ahead handsomely. There was nothing the two men could do in the time to stop her. Her bluff bows as inexorably as time approached the leaky gates and met them with a crunch that resounded in the lock. The onlookers eyes looked like a row of saucers as they uttered an incredulous 'Coo!' and the lockmaster jumped up and down as one of the gates gave way and the rush of water jammed the barge against the lock wall. Only the barge skipper appeared unmoved as he walked slowly up to the bows, surveyed the damaged gates, remarked, 'Wot's done can't be undone,' and walked aft again. The lock was out of use for weeks.

When at Eastertime a pal and I sallied forth from the lock we were delighted at the way *Afrina* handled now that she was no longer ballasted so much by the head. She carried only a little weather helm, and despite her straight keel and 14 ft-long bowsprit the old smack showed herself remarkably certain and quick in stays. You needed to push the tiller only 10 or 15 degrees to leeward to start her, and she would then turn through the wind's eye as you handled the jib sheets. To make her easier to sail with two, or even singlehanded if need be, I had fitted the forestaysail to work itself on a boom. The working jib, however, still had to be set standing on the iron traveller, for I found it was too big a sail to be furled successfully with the Wykeham Martin gear I had.

Although over a quarter of a ton of iron bars and scrap had been taken out of her *Afrina* was still as stiff as a church under sail, and much livelier on the helm and far less wet forward when punching to windward.

To make anchor work lighter, too, I had removed the traditional slow and cumbersome wooden barrel windlass with its handspikes and installed an easily turned capstan. With two turns round its upright barrel the heavy chain fed itself down into the locker below, so that there was no need to touch or range the cable as you hove it in with the capstan handles. When the anchor – a great 85 lb. fisherman – rose to the stemhead you reached down with the boathook, caught a bight of line spliced in the crown of the anchor, and swung the fluke up against the starboard rail (where the knightheads used to be in old-time ships and coasters) and lashed it there. Held fast thus with its stock athwart the stem under the bowsprit this Brittlesea fashion of carrying a fisherman-type anchor could hardly be bettered. The great thing was you never had to lift the whole weight of the anchor, as you do when you stow it inboard, and it was always ready for instant use – on occasion a vital factor in a ship with no engine.

Like Brightlingsea Creek, West Mersea had a fleet of about 30 smacks, and *Afrina* fitted well into the picture when she brought up in one of the creeks. The local smacksmen were a cheery lot and included some quaint characters who liked to tell a tall yarn. One day while I was anchored in the Quarters one of the oystermen from Packing Marsh Island came alongside in his punt evidently ready for a yarn as a tall rangy looking smacksman sailed past in his brig, a local heavy open oyster boat with a gaff sloop rig.

'That's young Lofty, that is,' said my visitor. 'Course, he warn't always as long as that.'

'Warn't he,' I echoed, 'I mean, he wasn't?' A glass of something warming was passed over the rail.

'Naw. His name's Ernie really, and he uster be medium 'igh like you and me, sir. Come a day though, when he was a grown lad, and he's out with his dad, owd Jessie we called him, in their owd smack. Down near the Bench Head, that's where they was a gooin' drudgin' that day, they sights a heavy owd bo't wot had gone adrift, same time as one or two of the others had seen 'er. Owd Jessie he was a rare one for smelling a bit o' salvage like, and he ups the hellum like lightning and runs down to this bo't. They ranges alongside just ahead of the other smack and still going a bit fast like he hollers out to young Ernie to pass a line through a ring in the bot's bow and make fast. But Ernie's a bit slow like – he was only a lad then – and he drops the end of the line. 'Grab 'er,' shouts owd Jessie, ''an' don't yew let go, bor!' Young Ernie grabs the bot's stempost and holds on. But she's a tidy weight, that owd bo't, and he feels hisself being pulled steady like over the smack's stern. His dad's at the tiller and hollerin' at another smack to git outer his way and don't turn to look at the boy. And Ernie dursn't say a word 'cause he was right scared of his dad, but he sees the other smack grab the bo'ts stern with a boathook and tail on, and when he was pulled overboard until he was holdin' onto the rail with only the toes of his boots he still dursn't let goo, for he knew he would only fall into the water and they'd lose the bo't and the salvage, and he reckoned he'd get a hidin' from his old man. And owd Jessie he nivver turns round till they was practically up at the Nass, and when he see young Ernie stretched out astern like a human bridge as you might say, he nearly dies o' laughin'. And I give you my word, sir, and it's gawd's truth as I sit 'ere, young Ernie had growed more'n six inches – he's been called Lofty ever since!'

With three aboard to share the work *Afrina* was one of the finest boats I ever had for ranging around the east coast. With her full body and false keel she would sit upright on any soft ground, while she would stand up to a capful of wind and roar along with her lee scuppers gurgling and only the occasional dollop of water flying over the weather rail to pour in a stream around the helmsman's boots. But crews were not always easy to obtain at short notice, and one or two weekends I sailed alone, and hard work it was. *Afrina*'s heavy mainsail, a job for a lone hand to stow, was set on a gaff 19 ft long, while her main-boom was 26 ft in length and 5½ in. in diameter at the after end. Taken slowly and carrying out the jobs in the right order getting the old smack underway from anchor could, I found, be done by one man of average height and strength, but it took half an hour's heavy effort. And with no engine to help, when it breezed up the work left one panting and played out, and I began to admit that I had indeed bitten off more than I could chew without a partner to share her, and *Afrina*, dear seakindly old ship though she was, had defeated me. It was plain I must keep to boats that I could handle alone without trying to rely on crews: would one ever learn?

Afrina was bought by a very likeable man with two hefty sons, who sailed her away to their home mooring on the South Coast. They wrote glowing letters of her fine behaviour in the longer Channel seas when the first season they sailed her 1200 miles to the West and back. After a few years they decided to have an engine installed, and while the old smack was on the hard in Chichester Harbour having the work done, the great gale of September 1935 which destroyed many yachts in the area drove several vessels ashore around *Afrina*, and the poor little ship was crushed and so damaged by the others as to be beyond repair. Like our old *Afrin* she had a sad finish to a long life.

Work in London was beginning to pile up. My second book, *The Magic of the Swatchways*, which had appeared in 1932, was selling fairly well – over the next thirty years it was to run into several editions – and I had already started writing a third. Increasing commissions for new yacht designs in addition made it necessary to burn the late-night oil at least three nights a week and to spend weekends over the drawing board. Such a programme gets a lot of work done, but is not good if kept up for too long. An internal weakness that has plagued me ever since those first few hungry years of freelance writing in London broke out again, and led to an illness that was slow to get rid of. The doctor advised a sea voyage!

Nevertheless the call of the Essex marsh winds and the feel of a leadline cool and wet in the hands was stronger than ever, and once more I felt that much of one's real happiness rested in a boat of one's own, a boat well within one's reduced strength. Early in the year, therefore, a chance enquiry led me to Acle, on the River Bure of all places, where in the gloom of a large boat shed, while a cold wind stretched its fingers across the Norfolk marshes, I came across an interesting white sloop. She was not exactly what I thought I wanted, but there were points about her worth looking at. Designed and built on Oulton Broad in 1910 – the year of *Storm* – specially for a man and his wife to sail on the Norfolk Broads or round the Suffolk coast, *Nightfall* had a superb cabin panelled in beech and mahogany with comfortable Vi-spring berth mattresses and back-rests covered in rich red pegamoid. There was standing headroom beneath a well-cambered cabin top and skylight, and at one side of the six-foot cockpit a single-cylinder two-stroke 6 horse-power Boulton and Paul motor of 1910 drove the central shaft by means of a cyclecar chain. The mast, balanced with lead weights Broads fashion, worked in a tabernacle, and the overall measurements, 31 ft length, 9 ft beam, gave her plenty of room below, while her draught of only 3 ft 3 in. with a long straight iron keel of two tons appealed strongly to me. Not by any means everybody's boat, too long in the keel for easy sailing on the Broads, too lightly built for sailing offshore, *Nightfall* had been laid up in this shed and for sale for more than two years. But I thought if I could buy her for a low enough price I could afford to make a ship of her suitable for these East Coast waters. A low offer was tried as an opening gambit and, to my surprise, was accepted.

Two of us left Lowestoft at dusk one weekend in April and sailed her round to the mooring off the clubhouse at Heybridge before very fresh easterly winds. The way she tossed and lurched and splashed along through the darkness, and the way the mast with no backstays bent forward, gave us some anxious moments, which were not in the least helped by the thought of the many

unlighted buoys marking banks off the shore that lay in our
path. It was in fact a very boisterous night, and despite our
boat's buoyancy and liveliness some of the crests broke along the
weather rail and slopped over our chilled bodies in the cockpit.

Happily we did not encounter any of the buoys which passed
unseen in the darkness (had we hit one our bows might have
been split open, and we had no dinghy with us on this trip) and
we made Heybridge next day tired but contented. We were less
happy later when it was learnt that the seas running up astern
had filled the engine exhaust system and the cylinder, the
engine had seized solid and could not be freed again. The poor
ruined old relic with its fascinating low-tension battery ignition
and direct reversing (like a steam engine) had to be taken out
and served the rest of its days permanently under water as
another boat's mooring. Thereupon I decided that as *Nightfall*
was so light to handle and manoeuvrable under sail or sweep I
would sail her without an engine for the time being. In the event
it was two years and several hundred miles of coastal cruising
later when I next succumbed to petrol power and fitted her with
a highly satisfactory engine out of an 11·9 horsepower Morris
Cowley (Bullnose) car.

Whenever I could get down to Heybridge *Nightfall* sailed up
and down the coast like a gull in flight, sometimes with friends,
more often singlehanded. Peter was no longer a shipmate, for
we had amicably agreed that our two courses did not run
parallel and in time she found happiness in another marriage,
this time to a celebrated marine artist. Meanwhile *Nightfall* gave
me all I needed then of a boat: she was roomy and comfortable
in her charming Edwardian cabin where the coal stove I installed
often cast a glowing warmth, she was easy for the lone hand to
manage, and whoever sailed in her was delighted with her speed.
By having the long broads-type forehatch and tabernacle closed
in, an anchor windlass fitted on the foredeck, three feet cut off
the end of the mainboom, Wykeham Martin furling jib and
forestaysail to manage itself on a boom and with extra oak
floors and some more frames fitted, *Nightfall* was turned into
quite a good-looking and practical little gaff cutter for these
turbulent Estuary waters.

Her long keel would enable her to keep on course with tiller lashed (with a slip knot) on a passage round the coast, while I busied myself with carpentry tools adding improvements to her interior. This ability to sail herself with helm temporarily fixed is one I have long demanded of any boat for the cruising man; and yachts of this long-keel type have no need for any complicated steering mechanism unless they are to run with winds on the quarter or right aft. Like much electronic equipment that clutters up small yachts' cabins these days, for many weekend yachts I have thought vane steering gear is mainly an owners' status symbol.

During the first two years I had *Nightfall* without an engine we ranged around the coast between Aldeburgh and the North Foreland and across to ports on the Belgian coast. One long Whitsun weekend an old school friend and I got caught out in a rising westerly gale while crossing the Estuary from the Crouch. Somewhere off the Mouse light, in the midst of a turmoil of very nasty breaking seas from the weather-going tide, the peak halyard span on the gaff parted and the gaff swung down. It was no fun getting the well-reefed sail down and the span repaired and sail reset while the ship was dancing like a shuttlecock, but we managed it, and were glad to slog our way into the Medway and bring up in the comparative quiet of Queenborough for the night. When we went ashore later, still feeling the effects of our rough passage, we went into a local store where a kind-faced woman served us. When she learnt that we had just sailed round from Burnham her eyes became misty behind her specs as she exclaimed: 'Oh, but that's *nice*! I've always longed for a nice quiet 'oliday on the water.' I only hope she didn't hear our laughter as we reeled along the pavement back to our ship, but after that whenever we have been at sea in rough and perhaps unnerving conditions we have been apt to repeat her '. . . a nice *quiet* 'oliday on the water!'

For nearly five years *Nightfall* continued to give me some of the happiest weekend cruising I can remember. Living now at Shenfield only a half-hour's journey to Liverpool Street for daily commuting to the *Yachting Monthly* office and a junction for the lines to all the Essex and Suffolk yachting anchorages, I usually went down to the boat by train so as to be able to return home from any of the ports where I had left her. It was like the carefree weekend cruising we had enjoyed ten years earlier.

Having by now designed for other owners a number of yachts of various sizes and types from 6 tons to 30 tons (*Ionia*, a centre-board ketch which was built in Alexandria for an official of an Egyptian bank) I began to feel the itch to design and build for my own use, and started to draft a set of lines. *Nightfall*'s days for me were accordingly numbered and with some sadness I sold her to an enthusiastic buyer, but the thought of building an entirely new boat at last was too attractive. Despite her sixty years *Nightfall* is still (1970) afloat and to be seen sailing on the East Coast. What immense pleasure, I often think, is given to so many owners and their friends and families by these long-lived yachts of amiable character, such as *Nightfall*, *Afrina*, *Storm*, *Puffin* and others known to all yachtsmen. Boats in their way are like old houses: they all vary in character and by their age and beauty they can bring peace and contentment to generations of those who can appreciate them.

The Sparkman and Stephens yawl *Dorade* had recently astonished British ocean-racing yachts by crossing the Atlantic in record time and then winning the Fastnet Cup from the best of our yachts. Details of her partly revolutionary design in terms of offshore racing impressed themselves on all the leading British yacht designers, and some of the ingenious ideas incorporated in her equipment were emulated. One of these was the box water-trap ventilator which became widely known as the Dorade vent. There followed in the years to come from the Sparkman and Stephens office a long line of highly successful ocean-racer designs which were direct developments of the original *Dorade*. These designs in their turn had a strong influence on all new ocean racers on both sides of the Atlantic, until indeed alterations in rating rules began to favour a different hull type, the shallow hull with short, deep fin-keel and separate rudder with or without trim tabs. Thus are the latest ideas in racing yacht forms outdated and superseded by ever new developments.

Whether it was this exciting influence by the remarkable Stephens brothers, Olin and Rod (which, of course, we reported in full in the *Yachting Monthly*) or a latent desire for just a

123

complete change from broad-shoal draught boats I don't know to this day. But the boat I next had built at Harry King's yard at Pin Mill in the winter of 1935–36 was a 10 ton yawl nearly 36 ft overall, with 9 ft 3 in. beam and drawing 5 ft, with a Parsons/ Ford 10 horse-power petrol motor. Although she was Bermudian rigged the old order for the lone cruising sailor remained in the Wykeham Martin jib set on a bowsprit and the forestaysail working on a boom. She had a counter stern that could by a stretch of imagination be described as resembling *Dorade*'s, but whatever the plans showed in the building of her the stern became thin and narrower at the taffrail than expected. A friend looking up at her in the building shed remarked: 'You might name her *Cassius*. She has a lean and hungry look!' But I called her *Wild Lone II*.

And when I watched her being launched I found myself like, I suspect, many a bridegroom, asking: 'Good heavens, M. G., what *have* you done? She's not a bit your type!'

11. *America for good ideas?*

In bygone times it was an accepted aspect of upper-class life that a man – fictionally described as the whiskered, tophatted, portly, august pater familias – would employ an architect to build him a solid and pretentious house which was intended to serve as the family home for generations to come. The building of the house was to be an emotional as well as a financial experience that would last for the rest of papa's life, for he would never build another. For some yachtsmen the decision to have a yacht designed and built specially for them results in a similar emotional upheaval, and one to be enjoyed once in their yachting lives.

This steadiness of purpose and faithfulness to one house or one yacht is a highly admirable quality that I have at times envied, but it is one I have not yet been able to share. My mother, who had some Celtic blood in her veins and was active and alert almost to the day of her death at 92, had a fertile imagination and detested the restraint of humdrum routine. I dare say I have inherited some of her volatile qualities that infuriated poor father. 'Go on, try anything once,' was often her advice and from time to time she would adopt wholeheartedly any current craze that was outside the hated domestic life. Votes for women (a vehement suffragette in her day), palmistry, occultism, theosophy, astrology and other ologies gave her wide interests that made her conversation anything but dull for her frequently shocked friends. One day when she was 82 she announced that she wanted to be taken flying before she died, not in one of those airliners but in an open plane so she could see where she was going and could feel the wind on her face. On a fine day an old sailing friend of mine who had a small plane with an open cockpit took her up for a short flight. When she stepped down from the tiny machine and collapsed on the field we thought we'd done it that time. But all she said

125

was: 'Oh, it's only excitement in my legs. But it's *marvellous* up there. If only I was ten years younger I'd take flying lessons!' It is perhaps little wonder that we never lived in any house for more than a few years and that I grew up used to change, so that I have tended to experiment with my boats rather than to remain faithful to one for many long years.

Before any new vessel, yacht, coaster, tug, trawler, train ferry or passenger ship is launched even the most experienced designer is apt to have butterflies in the tummy as she goes down into the water and he wonders if all the calculations were correct and she will float on the right marks. No one knows for certain how a new design of plane will fly, until it has flown; and no one has yet been able to predict with certainty how a new design of sailing yacht will behave until she has been sailed. Air and water are fluid media and the effects of their powerful forces on different shapes of hull and rigs can be almost unpredictable.

Some vessels, and not only yachts, have been badly out of trim or have floated far deeper than as calculated when they were launched. At one large yacht yard on the South Coast I once attended a crowded launching ceremony for a new ocean racer from the board of a celebrated designer. When she slid down the slipway the yacht floated nine inches too deep by the stern. A chunk of lead from the after end of her ballast keel had to be cut out, recast and stowed as far forward as could be before her racing career began. One builder who had never before produced anything larger than a 20-footer, the story was told me, was completing a yacht of about 8 tons for a fussy customer. The launching date having been announced and a number of the builder's sceptical friends having promised to come, the builder became so worried that she might not float anywhere near his marks and his carefully painted waterline might be inches out, that he could almost hear the laughter of his headshaking friends. One night he accordingly let her go quietly down the slip, marked the line on the hull where she floated, hauled her out again, and next day painted in the waterline. And on the day of the launch his astonished friends congratulated him on his air of quiet confidence and sang-froid as his yacht slid into the water and the painted line was exactly right!

As it turned out *Wild Lone* II was out of trim by only two inches at the stern, but this did not seem to affect her adversely and those of us who sailed in her were pleased with the balance on the helm and her general handiness. But from the cransiron on her bowsprit to the end of her mizzen boom she was almost 49 ft from tip to tip, even a little longer than *Afrina*, and when I was singlehanded she did prove something of an embarrassment when working in and out of a crowded anchorage. Her draught also caught me out in unexpected places, and more than once I found myself spending hours perched on the edge of the cabin settee at an angle of 50 degrees as in the days of *Undine*. Would one, I asked once again, ever learn?

The America's Cup races when Tom Sopwith challenged with his second *Endeavour* were held in September 1937, and the proprietors of the *Yachting Monthly* gave me a month's leave to go to Newport, Rhode Island, to cover the races for the magazine. This promised to be not only a welcome relief from the editorial desk and the telephone, but a visit to the United States would enable me to advance my study of shallow-draught centreboard yachts in the land of their origin. It was indeed a wonderful experience, for I had already been in correspondence with a number of well-known American yacht designers while working on a book on shallow-draught yachts which was later published by Peter Davies in London and Yachting Inc. in New York with the title *Little Ships and Shoal Waters*.

In the cordial American manner I was enabled to meet prominent names in yachting like Alf Loomis, Olin and Rod Stephens, Herbert Stone, editor of New York *Yachting*, and shortly before his death at the age of 90 I was able to talk with the blind Nat Herreschoff, perhaps America's most celebrated designer of beautiful yachts. Hours spent in the fascinating models room of the New York Yacht Club followed by long discussions with architects who had specialized in designs for centreboarders encouraged me in thinking I was on the right track in my ideas for sea-going yachts of shallow draught. An old correspondent, Henry Howard, then in his 70s, showed me the very detailed drawings of his cleverly designed *Alice*. This handsome 52 ft centreboard gaff ketch with 13·6 ft beam and 4 ft draught had been designed for Mr Howard in 1923 by Commodore Munro of Coconut Grove, Florida, a celebrated designer of shoal-draught craft of all kinds as well as of lifeboats for the U.S. Bureau of Shipping. With his wife and family the owner had cruised along the Eastern Seaboard between Newport, their home, and the Bahamas, their other base, a number of times, and the *Alice* with board raised had ridden out more than one gale and the tail of a hurricane. His book describing her building which appeared in 1926 was reprinted with additional material in 1946 by Dodd Mead of New York as *The Yacht Alice, Twenty Years After*, and is a classic on the sea-going qualities of the lifeboat type of centreboarder.

Returning home aboard the M.S. *Georgic* (within four years, in 1941, I was to fly over her burning bomb-blasted hull in a Navy plane while she lay aground in the Bay of Suez) I started to draft a new set of lines for a 28 ft centreboarder which I had already decided to have built as soon as I had sold my present boat. Not entirely logically, the ideas that had presented themselves with *Swan*, of a shallow hull with fixed leeboards, or bilge keels, never entered my head as I discussed centreboarders with my American friends and thought out plans for my new boat. Yet I had heard about Robin Balfour's original *Bluebird* and had accepted for inclusion in my *Little Ships and Shoal Waters* book, the plans of another ingenious twin bilge keel sloop, *Buttercup*, which had been designed by Robert Clark in London. Neither innovation just then nudged me into thinking that instead of a centreboard I could try twin keels in my next boat; I guess I must have been swathed in a comfortable centreboard fixation.

Wild Lone ii found an appreciative buyer who took her to his home in Scotland and cruised extensively in her for years around the Western Isles. He was delighted with her and sent heart-warming letters describing how well the yawl behaved in the tough conditions of his beloved West Coast. Later when she changed hands again she spent many years based in Northern Ireland, cruising around the Irish coasts and one year sailing down to the Mediterranean and back.

7. *Witchcraft*, a fine example of a *Y.M.* 30-ft. Waterwitch (W 49)

Photo: Alan Bond

There seemed to be nothing wrong with her as a capable offshore cruising boat, and a sister ship built at Burnham for Sir Carne Rasch was sailed regularly across to Holland and around Home Waters for more than thirty years until her owner died. I had made the mistake thinking that a yacht of *Wild Lone* II's length and draught could be an entirely happy choice for the modest kind of ditchcrawling that I found I enjoyed most: another of my mistakes!

Lone Gull, the new boat, was built by Johnson and Jago at Leigh-on-Sea on the north shore of the Thames Estuary during the winter of 1937–38. She measured 28·4 ft in length with 10 ft beam and 3 ft 3 in. draught, and was cutter rigged with Bermudian mainsail, forestaysail on a boom, and Wykeham Martin jib. The centreboard, L-shaped with lifting chain at the after end, was built up from 2 in. oak planks and iron shod round its edges. The forward part of its case was flush with the wide cabin floor, the after part was carried up to the cabin top beams and formed a convenient fore and aft bulkhead enclosing a pleasing galley to port. The engine, a 20 horsepower 4-cylinder Grey motor, was installed to starboard of the centreboard case and drove the central propeller shaft through a silent chain enclosed in a case.

Lone Gull proved herself a very stiff and handy boat, capable like *Storm* and *Nightfall* of lying hove-to quietly or sailing herself indefinitely with tiller pegged, and easy if somewhat heavy to handle alone. With various friends I spent weekends happily cruising about the East Coast, and explored the upper reaches of creeks in the Medway, the Swale and the Alde River where I had never penetrated before. We never took her far for I had found that with weekend sailing a summer holiday was of far less benefit than one taken in mid-winter, and for some years I boarded a ship in December or January and spent two weeks at sea or in Portugal with friends and one year I went to Finland in February. I had come to realize that too much obsession with small boats could deprive one of the benefits of foreign travel.

On the whole *Lone Gull* was very much the type of sturdy, capable East Coast centreboarder with a distinct American influence in her beam and hull form that then pleased me enormously. But in a mood of honest criticism of my own work I had to admit that her design revealed several faults. Although the centreboard case arrangement with the enclosed galley was an attractive and convenient layout, I found it placed the board rather too far aft, and this resulted in only a mediocre windward performance: she needed a better bite at the water to work faster to windward. To fit in the powerful Grey engine I had had to fill in the run aft more than I liked, and in consequence she was not nearly so fast as *Nightfall* on any point of sailing. Her decks were of tongue-and-groove pine canvas covered (the last I would ever have of this old form of deck) and the mast was stepped through the cabin top on to the keel. If the rigging was not always kept bar taut the movement of the mast in breezy weather strained the cabin top first to port and then to starboard. As a result it seemed well nigh impossible to keep the joint between the carlines and coamings from leaking. The side decks were so low that little use could be made of the space beneath them except for lockers. Raised topsides amidships, I decided, would give one much more space here at the sides of the cabin, and with unbroken deck beams would avoid leaky deck joints.

There were four yachts eventually built to *Lone Gull*'s plans and one of them went out to the West Indies. In other designs based on this one raised midship decks were fitted with a large main hatch to give 6 ft headroom, and a number of yachts have been built to these plans in various parts of the world.

Before the second season with *Lone Gull* ran to a close, events in Europe were marching towards destruction of life as we then knew it. I arranged to have the boat laid up in the yard where she had been built and the engine removed and put in store. She lay alongside another design of mine, the ketch *Kanwara* of 19 tons T.M., which had just been built for a client who had already had two other yachts built from my plans. The launching date for *Kanwara* had been postponed, for it was September 1939.

My old colleague Norman Clackson and I were already in the R.N. Volunteer Supplementary Reserve and our efforts to prepare the *Yachting Monthly* for what was to come were cut short by our being called up. Miss Kathleen Palmer, who had been with the firm fourteen years, was left to carry on with whatever assistance she could find, and did so through the six years of blackout and restrictions that followed. It was a proud claim that the old Y.M. did not miss a single issue throughout either the First World War or the Hitler conflict.

12. *Little ships of war*

'MINE Recovery Flotilla F Three to proceed forthwith to Ramsgate. Lieut. Griffiths report on arrival.'

So read the signal on a day in 1940. 'You know what that means, Griffiths,' said the Duty Commander at the Naval Base at Dundee. 'Dunkirk. Good luck.'

In line ahead as if we really were a smart flotilla of warships my group of insignificant North Sea trawlers left the mouth of the Tay and wended their way south along the coast, keeping a mile or two offshore but inside the limits of the minefields, my own trawler *Sailor King* in the van as pilot. Each was supposed to have been rendered non-magnetic, and all four of them were equipped with special non-magnetic gear to deal with the German parachute-dropped ground mines wherever they could be found. But this operation, we had been told, would be something different.

As first the tall finger of Orfordness light and then the distant Naze passed abeam, and we steamed into the Black Deep with our eyes on the clear sky looking for enemy aircraft and saw the dark line of the North Foreland come up over the horizon, I felt we were back home in waters I knew well. But in the harbour at Ramsgate, seething with small craft of all kinds from motor boats to a paddle steamer as they disgorged their crowds of refugees on to the quays, an anticlimax dampened our long-held excitement. The days of Dunkirk were drawing to a close, and an order had just been received from the Admiralty stopping all vessels with a speed of less than 15 knots from making any further trips to the beaches.

Even with their funnels glowing red and their ventilators shaking in unison like nervous swans the best speed my little ships could make in calm water was 9½ knots, and even if we had tried to claim a fictional fifteen we were told in no uncertain terms at Navy Office that with 12½ ft we drew far too much

anyway, and who the hell had ordered four bloody trawlers to
come barging in now etc. etc. etc. Badly disappointed and with
our tails so to speak between our legs, yet thankful that by this
time almost all the troops had apparently been ferried across
the Channel and were safe again on England's soil, we took our
instructions to return forthwith to our Base on the Tay.

Routed in a large convoy from the anchorage off Southend as
far as abreast Harwich, our quartet of smoky Joes continued on
their own way north, putting into Grimsby because three of the
trawlers needed coal, and doubtless purely coincidentally two
of our skippers and their crews were Grimsby men. A few hours
later, with bunkers full of good Welsh stuff and less smoke from
our funnels, the four of us left the Humber in a flat calm, still
in line ahead with our high bows lifting and falling over an
almost imperceptible swell, and steamed slap into a dense fog
that closed in at dusk as we were abreast the mouth of the Tyne.
Unsuspecting, our course led us through the middle of an out-
ward-bound convoy, and as first one giant black shape loomed
out of the gathering gloom on our port bow and then another
and another, slipping past our bows and stern in complete
blackout darkness and silence but for the low wash of their
bow waves and the throb of engines, we took rapid avoiding
action, goggle-eyed with our hats standing up on our scalps.
Yet not one angry voice blasted us from the bridge of any of
these mysterious monsters: these Merchant Service chaps, I
thought, must either be amazingly polite or else they were
rendered silent thinking we were a flotilla of German U-boats.

When the last ship had disappeared and we seemed to have
the sea to ourselves again I had our fog drill put into immediate
operation. From *Sailor King* in the lead we payed out a small
dan buoy on a hundred-fathom line from our stern while the
other trawlers closed station, the second and third ships doing
the same. Without being allowed any lights it was the best we
could do, although a lot to expect of even young seamen's eyes
to keep sight of a small buoy being towed ahead of their ships'
bows. I knew none of our skippers would want to wander too far
offshore to the eastward, as continuous minefields lay roughly
three miles from the coast, and I hoped none of them would try
to close the coast too much and put their trawlers ashore. Like

a school marm with a crocodile of girls trying to hold hands I led the four little ships on through the fog on a course that I reckoned kept us roughly two miles off the beach. All night long we maintained our steady 8 knots while our up-and-down compound engines kept up their slow rhythm to the gentle wash of our bow wave. Sometimes on the pilot bridge within the welcome warmth of the funnel, at others pacing up and down the deck between the trawl winch and the galley aft, I was kept awake with mugs of thick sweet trawler tea, telling myself, 'I must savour every minute of this. It is *steam yachting*, and I'll never be able to afford anything like this again.' And though we had never got to Dunkirk, nor gallantly saved a single soldier, we had to admit it had been one hell of a fine cruise!

By dawn, with the fog as thick as ever and the bows of the *Scotch Thistle* just visible close up astern with her nose on our buoy (I blessed her trusting skipper) straining ears heard the faint wail of the Lindisfarne foghorn away to port, the first sound from land that had come to us all night. With a sigh of relief we felt we could now alter our course 12 degrees to port straight for the Bell light off the mouth of the Tay. Our prayers were for this fog to clear with the rising sun, for I could not help thinking of the court martial that would follow if we grounded our *Sailor King* and the three other ships closed up on us like the wagons of a loose-coupled goods train. And almost at midday, as the warm sun began to eat up the mist, the first thing we sighted since we had lost the convoy in the fog the previous evening was the white finger of Bell Rock light right over the bow about 8 miles. These Abertay rocks marked the entrance to our river, and like many another mariner before me I thought with gratitude of

> The good old Abbot of Aberbrothock
> Who'd placed the Bell on the Inchcape Rock.

That long hot summer of 1940, so hideously wasted in the horror of making war, saw our scruffy little trawlers moved from the Dundee Base to Lowestoft for a continuation of their recovery work in the approaches to Harwich. To me Lowestoft was a highly interesting and enjoyable base. I could not have

asked for a more engrossing duty for an amateur than to have to
work a small steam trawler in and out of the fish dock and the
outer harbour with its double turn. Great care was needed to
enter the narrow passage between the piers where on both the
flood and ebb the tide poured past them like a millrace. One
minesweeper misjudged the angle of approach on a spring ebb
one day, was carried athwart the lee pier head and sank, partly
blocking the fairway. Raised hands in N.O.I.C.'s office and
some hot telephoning brought a salvage tug from Harwich and
the offending carcase was removed in 48 hours, but the merry
port was closed for that time and many of the trawler crews
thought they ought to have been granted a 48-hour 'lief' in lieu.

In the fish dock itself our trawlers were packed with their
minesweeping gear and other more secret equipment almost as
tightly as the steam drifters used to be before the war, and
working in and out of narrow berths without buckling the
stem or denting the taffrail showed just how handy a single-
screw steamer with a big slow turning screw can be in tight
quarters. By going slow ahead, then half astern, slow ahead,
half astern, wheel to port, wheel to starboard, over and over,
these single-screw handy little ships could be made to turn
round in the middle of the dock, then go stern first into a space
between two others with a foot or two to spare on each side. It
was all wonderful practice for the amateur Wavy Navy chap
who imagined this was his own steam yacht. Well, why not?

During a temporary lull in the mining of the channels in the
Thames Estuary two of the ships of my flotilla with their special
lifting gear were ordered to carry out a piece of salvage work.
One of our bombers returning from a raid over Germany had
come down in the sea in shallow water off the beach at Corton,
a few miles north of Lowestoft, and the R.A.F. was anxious to
retrieve some secret part of the equipment. In this interesting
operation I was lent the assistance of an engaging and energetic
young R.N.V.R. Lieutenant, Rex S., who was a trained mine
rendering safe (M.R.S.) officer and also had experience of
salvage, as before the war he had managed his own salvage
company on the Mersey. We liked one another from the start,
finding this type of work together highly congenial, and after
effecting another small salvage job we talked of joining forces

135

in a salvage and ferry business after the war. It began to look as if life would eventually be more in the open air with the sea as a challenge instead of at an office desk in London, and I seriously considered the prospect offered an interesting future.

Not long after Rex was sent to Falmouth with a diving party to deal with a parachute mine which had been dropped in the harbour and was holding up ship movements. He had learnt Naval-type diving for his company in peace time, and after his diver had come up and reported that the mine below was very large and looked a bit different, he put on the dress and went down to see for himself. It is thought that this was one of the first of the acoustic mines dropped by the Germans. These had a sensitive mechanism set to be actuated by the reverberations of a passing ship's propellor, but could also be set off by any prolonged noise such as the air escaping from a nearby diver's helmet or even his lead boot scraping against the shell of the mine. Whatever the cause the mine went up, killing Rex and his diving boat's crew, and injuring a number of men aboard a harbour boat lying some distance off. We had known others of our M.R.S. officers and men who had been killed by mines, but the loss of Rex and his party came as a particularly bad shock, reminding us that the war was not over yet.

The Germans once more stepped up their mine dropping, no doubt as new supplies came from their factories, and our flotilla was kept busy in conjunction with the other mine sweepers in trying to keep the ship channels clear. Between hours of acute anxiety and moments of sudden fright from aircraft attack life was hard but on the whole good. Each of my trawlers had her own fishing skipper and I had now been able to sort out the good men, who were excellent types, from the mediocre and hopeless, and we had all their crews trained to a state of keen efficiency. It was altogether a fully satisfying period, for I know of nothing better for a man than to be one of a happy ship's company, nor any body of men more likely to keep cheerful and hard-working under trying conditions than a detail of Naval ratings under the eye of a good petty officer. In H.M. ships, at least in small ships in wartime, which were the extent of my own experience, there was a wonderful sense of the sharing together the life of the ship and its discomforts and

136

dangers, ('we're all in the same boat' is a saying not without significance) and this easy understanding throughout a small ship's company might well derive from the days when Francis Drake laid down the rule that in his fighting ships there was no room for inactive passengers. 'The mariners,' he decreed, 'shall haul with the gentlemen, and the gentlemen with the mariners.'

But it was not all joyous, for one of our trawlers when working on a magnetic mine in a shallow channel off Margate touched it off and disappeared completely in a great mound of mud and spray. There were no survivors. And another was run into by a big freighter at night when returning from an operation, and damaged beyond repair, happily with no casualties. Our hard-working little flotilla was now reduced to two ships only, *Scotch Thistle* and *Sailor King*. But by now the Admiralty had the measure of the enemy's magnetic mine, counteracted with the degaussing of ships, the successful Double-L sweep and other measures, and there was less work for our mine recovery flotillas to do.

An Admiralty message that I had been given an extra half stripe as Lieut.-Commander meant an immediate change in my appointment once more, and I had to say farewell to the excellent ship's company who had taught their Wavy Navy Lieutenant so much in so short a time. But the sadness of relinquishing this minor command in the Thames Estuary was balanced soon after by some elation (and a party with a dreadful hangover) when another message announced that my name was amongst those of other officers of the mine recovery service who had been awarded the George Medal.

Posted to Whale Island in Portsmouth Harbour for a crash course in diving – traditional Naval fashion, lead boots and weights, rubber suit, brass helmet, the lot – in one week I became qualified in theory to take charge of special diving parties in order to be able to deal with magnetic ground mines under water. Still somewhat deaf from the earcracking course and at a few hours' notice, I found myself with my diving party, all first-rate fellows, in a plane on the way to Egypt. An overnight flight of 13 hours by stripped Wellingtons to Malta, followed next night by a second hop to Abu Sweir airfield, shot

137

us from the snow and ice of a hard January in England into the oven-hot wind of the desert by Ismailia. The Nazis had been dropping their parachute mines into the Suez Canal and two ships had already been sunk.

Our orders were to clear all mines out of the Canal and, where possible, render safe and send the mechanisms back to the experts at the *Vernon*, Portsmouth, in case Teutonic ingenuity was making mine-sweeping ineffective. We were also to organize a mine-watching service. At first this appeared a stupendous task for some one hundred miles of Canal, and an idea from some misguided but very high authority to cover the whole Canal at night with nets, so that a dropping mine would reveal its position by leaving a hole, was so impracticable that it had to be gently but firmly thrust aside. It would drain all the jute from India, take weeks to make, and when lowered to the canal bed as the authority proposed, it would, we submitted, wrap itself firmly round the ship's propellers in the very shallow water. We won our day and in the end enlisted the co-operation of the Egyptian Army. Soldiers were stationed at watching posts about every half mile down the length of the Canal to report any parachute seen during a raid, and by means of a movable pointer on a wooden dial to mark the position where it fell. I came to like these cheerful brown-faced men, for they never failed to get a bearing, often two together, on a mine drop, and the whole system worked quite efficiently. Watching them made me want to come back to Egypt when the war was over and before I got back to a job and see something of this fascinating country and the history of these interesting people.

But right now we had other matters on our hands. It was at the time of the invasion of Greece, and on one occasion my divers and the demolition crew had been under several days of great strain. They knew how sensitive these mines could be, and the minutes while they worked below the diving boat and we in the boat waited for their reports seemed very long ones indeed. The Germans had blitzed Ismailia and during the riad had dropped a number of mines in the Canal, and a merchant ship had been sunk blocking the Narrows south of the Bitter Lakes. We had been told that the Greeks were desperate for military supplies and oil, and that their railways had coal for only another 48 hours. The salvage parties had moved the sunken ship a few yards and dug a narrow channel out of the side of the Canal, and North-bound supply ships, massed in Suez Bay, were already starting on their slow crawl through the Canal.

Working all night in the dark water my party located and detonated the last mine, we were able to report the channel open, and soon the first of the ships was agitating the water at our feet almost a quarter of a mile ahead of her bluff bows. As she slid slowly past, a rusty collier deep laden with the precious coal, followed by a tanker with aviation fuel, and then a long line of them stretching away to the South as far as the eye could see, the salvage and diving units gave a hearty cheer, while I found myself standing behind them on the bank with the tears running unashamedly down my face.

On a visit to the Naval Base in Alexandria I managed to take a few hours off to see something of this ancient Greek outpost. At the Yacht Club the Commodore, Colin Marshall, met me and showed me his 46 ft centreboard ketch *Ionia*, which I had designed for him ten years before. She was hauled out and spending the war under cover, and although he had sailed her with his trusty paid hand each year around the Greek Islands and the Eastern Mediterranean (his intimate knowledge here was proving of great service to the Admiralty) *Ionia* was so beautifully maintained by the faithful Ismail that she looked as if she had never been near the water. 'She's my dream ship,' Marshall told me. 'She has never had an engine, she is so easy to handle we have never felt the need for any power. After the war, Griffiths, why not come out to Egypt and come for a cruise with us to the beautiful Ionian Islands. I could also show you some of the treasures there are in Egypt that the ordinary tourist cannot see.' It was indeed a tempting thought, for Marshall had lived in Egypt most of his life and was a keen historian, but alas, he died soon after the war and I never had the opportunity to see him again.

A bout of malaria followed by dysentery in the Canal zone all but ended my terrestrial progress for ever, and still groggy from its effects I was despatched homeward, together with some returning R.A.F. ferry pilots, in a Sunderland flying boat. This lovely crate flew us southward up the Nile by way of Khartoum,

Lake Victoria, across Central Africa, down the great Congo River to the West Coast and Lagos. After eight days in Lagos, where I was delighted to meet an old school friend and get in a little sailing at the local club, another plane flew the party north by way of Lisbon (where we were allowed only in civilian clothes) home to old England. Once again I felt I must savour every hour of this long flight from Egypt, every sight as we touched down, for never again I felt sure would I be able to afford to fly so far nor to experience so much of this fascinating world.

Back again after a tiresome sick leave to Portsmouth and the *Vernon*, I was transferred from interest in enemy mines to explosives and demolition, and went through an absorbing period of training and research into the effects of special explosive charges on ships' plating. We became quite expert in punching any required size of hole from a foot in diameter to three feet or so through any steel plating which might vary between half an inch and seven eights of an inch according to the size of the ship. There was, unhappily, no shortage of wrecks at that time available for our tests.

Arising out of this I was appointed Vernon officer in charge of a number of demolition parties, each under a trained R.N.V.R. lieutenant, who were involved in fitting specially designed explosive charges to 77 different ships. These ships ranged in size from an old but very pretty Norwegian steamer of 5,500 tons to an ex-German liner of 17,500 tons. They were of various nationalities including French, Dutch, Greek, Panamanian and American merchant ships as well as four condemned warships, the French battleship *Courbet*, the Dutch cruiser *Sumatra*, and H.M. ships *Centurion* and *Durban*. One poor wreck I recall vividly. She was one of Kaiser's war-produced Liberty ships which had met an Atlantic gale on her maiden crossing with vital war stores and had broken her back, but by good fortune had been able to limp into port. The rents in her plating amidships had been roughly sewn together with bent railway iron in one of our dockyards, and they looked like giant zip fasteners down her sides. 'You'll hardly need any scuttling charges, old girl,' was my thought as we passed her in our launch.

Secret instructions given us were that all these ships were to be sunk in shallow water somewhere off a beach, and the requirement was for holes to be blown in them so that they would flood evenly and settle in a given number of minutes on an even keel; they must not show any tendency, as many ships do on sinking, to turn over on their sides. It seemed at first a difficult order, but our months of experiment and research stood us in good stead and our demolition parties were skilled men and to be relied upon. Given a fairly free hand by the Admiralty we had hundreds of explosive charges made to our own design, and our parties working below decks fitted them in pairs against the hull plating, one on the port side, one to starboard in each watertight compartment. According to the size and construction of each ship the number of charges varied from 12 to about 24, all interconnected so that they blew more or less simultaneously.

This work entailed my making frequent visits over many months to some twenty different ports and shipyards in England, the Clyde and Northern Ireland, and I grew well accustomed to clambering down iron ladders deep into the dark and cavernous holds of the merchant ships, through propeller-shaft tunnels and beneath boiler-room plates. The antique Free French battleship *Courbet* with her countless separate compartments like dark catacombs and $1\frac{1}{4}$ in. thick hull plating presented a problem at first, but on urgent request the Admiralty obtained for us some plans of her and then all seemed simple – more or less.

To save endless travelling time to all these scattered ports it was necessary for me to fly, but there was always a dearth of Naval planes for odd flights like these. Through an old sailing and pre-war flying friend (the same distinguished personality who had flown my mother at 82) who was an official in the Air Transport Auxiliary, the service that delivered planes from factory to airbases, a private plane was made available at any time with a pilot – who was as often as not a charming girl. The hard-pressed *Vernon* had reason to be grateful for the help Arnold Watson rendered with this wonderfully efficient air service, while the Wavy Navy chap could not have enjoyed it more!

By June 1944 when the seventy-seven old write-offs and many hundreds of other ships finally assembled to form what later became known as the Mulberry Harbours for the Normandy Invasion* the reason for our work became clear. And when the day came it was nevertheless a relief to learn that as each of our ships was manoeuvred into position, with her bow against the stern of the next ship ahead to form a sheltering outer breakwater, all the charges detonated correctly and the tired old ladies ended their sea careers and settled quietly on the bottom as planned. How the harbours were then speedily built and the greatest military invasion of all time proceeded almost without a hitch, and how from the beaches of Normandy the Allied Forces went on to liberate the peoples of Europe from the Nazi yoke is well-documented military history.

To the *Vernon* once again, nothing loth, for I had grown to love old Pompey, the Navy man's Portsmouth, but this time in one of their book-making establishments to assist in the rewriting of the Navy's outdated demolition drillbook. Back again, it seemed, to wrestle with paperwork, proofs and printers ink, as if they had been following me like a spectre all the time. But a pleasanter side to backroom life intervened. One day after lunch in the *Vernon* wardroom a voice asked 'Griff, have you met our new Wren officer?' Her name was Marjorie Copson , appointed to *Vernon* to assist in the command of five hundred Wrens, a hundred of them the admirable Boat Wrens, and when over the top of my *Telegraph* I met her quizzical eyes I thought of that haunting song:

> Some enchanted evening, you will see a stranger,
> You will see a stranger across a crowded room,
> And somehow you'll know, you'll know even then
> You will see her again and again . . . .

Marjorie and I were married in Portsmouth at the end of the year and the officers of the *Vernon* made it a full Naval ceremony. My wife's Boat Wrens brought us in a picket boat to the *Vernon* steps where more of her girls crossed oars over us before we were welcomed aboard by the Captain. And as we left for a brief

* The *The Last Passage,* by J. E. Taylor, Allen & Unwin, 1946.

honeymoon colleagues of my explosives group gave a demonstration that scared us all.

On being demobilized in 1945 we took stock of our position. In the years before the war I had published five yachting books and three novels, and in the manner of books each had its short run and then more or less withered away, with the exception of *The Magic of the Swatchways* which was still selling in fresh editions. A livelihood gained in writing books, although tempting as it offered a measure of freedom, would only too obviously lead to near starvation. I had also designed about 30 yachts, but immediate post-war conditions did not look promising either for the yacht designer.

Yet truth to tell, after the six years of excitement and travel experienced in the war I was very reluctant to return to the old daily routine of commuting on the 8.10 to the London office and to be tied once more to an editor's desk and its worries. It would be wiser, I thought, if I made yachting only an absorbing hobby instead of my whole occupation, and for a time I was tempted by a job in the research department of one of the big railway groups. It was perhaps fortunate that we decided against this attractive work, for the job would probably have terminated with the nationalization of the railways in 1948.

In the end common sense prevailed and I went back to the life of the commuter, to the editorial job which had been kept open, and once more took over the wheel of the *Yachting Monthly* with my old colleagues Norman Clackson and Kathleen Palmer. It was to be for a spell that lasted for the next twenty-two years.

Marjorie and I were fortunate that my house at Shenfield had survived all the bombing and our home was intact, and that *Lone Gull* had been cared for throughout the war by Len Johnson and Jimmy Jago. Despite a very near bomb crater during one of the raids she had emerged in good shape.

'Funny to think,' said Marjorie, whose home had been in Northamptonshire where her main love had been the countryside and riding, 'I always imagined that I'd eventually marry a farmer. Now I'm married to a yachtsman I'll just have to learn to like sailing, shan't I?'

And to her credit, when we commissioned *Lone Gull* again

Marjorie hid her natural fear of the sea and discovered that weekend sailing and cruising around the coast in a powerful boat, if taken quietly, had many aspects we could both enjoy. It was only the winds and the waves that did not always co-operate as one hoped they might.

Vahan, 2 tons

13. *In the lee of the sands*

LEARNING to get back into the routine of the five-day-a-week commuter from Shenfield, while Marjorie at home gave rein to her inborn aptitude for turning a dull Edwardian house into a warm and attractive domicile, I returned to paperwork like so many other ex-Service people only reluctantly. But in the evenings and over weekends in winter I was to produce four more yachting books and a number of new yacht designs over the next few years. Most weekends in summer we went aboard *Lone Gull* which was kept on a mooring in Besom Creek ('the Bussum') at West Mersea, 37 miles by road. A holiday cruise in *Lone Gull* to Holland with Marjorie and my old Mersea marine artist friend Fid Harnack, which included ten days with Dutch friends cruising around the Ijselmeer (the polder-enclosed Zuider Zee) in *Johanna*, an aged fishing botter, marked our 1947 season with a highlight. On the passage home Marjorie took the 2000 hours to midnight trick at the tiller while Fid and I slept below, and *Lone Gull* kept her lonely course across the mine fields, and although perhaps thinking of her quiet countryside and her horses Marjorie discovered for herself something of the fascination of a soft and gentle night at sea. Happily the weather remained quiet all the way back to Mersea.

The next year an old medico friend, Bill E. and I had a week sailing together across the Estuary, and as time and weather ran out for both our jobs in London we were forced to return home by train. He joined me again the following weekend to get her back to Mersea. As this little trip shows how advantageous it can be for a small yacht to make use of the shelter to be gained from the sands of the Thames Estuary, and how to do so you must have a suitable tough boat of quite shallow draught, here is the story of this passage. I call it 'In the Lee of the Sands'.

It was not as though Bill and I had all the time in the world. *Lone Gull* was in Ramsgate, where we had left her the weekend before, and the forecast spoke of north-easterly winds moderate to fresh. These were not the best conditions for crossing the Estuary from south to north, but we were anxious to get our trusty old centreboarder back to her moorings in the Black-water.

When my able crew and I took her out between the piers in the early morning the wind lay a little more easterly than as forecast, and as *Lone Gull* punched into the lumpy seas off the pierheads it began to look as though we should be able to lay our course to the North East Spit buoy and so on to the Edin-burgh Channel. The last of the north-going tide was helping us along, and soon the North Foreland began to open out to port.

'Wind seems to be backing a little,' Bill remarked as he sat with one arm crooked over the tiller and peered through his spectacles at the bulkhead compass. 'I can't quite lay the North East Spit.'

Glancing around the sky to windward I sensed that this wind was going to back still further, perhaps to north of north east. That would make the long leg through the South Edinburgh Channel, across Black Deep into the Barrow Deep and on into the Swin a very slow passage with the spring flood tide about to run partly against our course. With the chart of the Thames Estuary on the cabin table I did some rapid calculations while the little ship sidled and curtseyed on her way, and Bill left the helm pegged and joined me in the cabin.

'Tell you what we'll do, Bill,' I said at length. 'We'll square away and take this fair tide and wind with us through Margate Roads and the Gore Channel to the Hook beacon, and then strike across the Kentish Flats and the Oaze Deep into the West Swin near the Mouse lightvessel. It should be getting near high water by then, and as this is a good spring tide there ought to be enough water over the Maplins for us to slip into Havengore creek with our board up. I'll ease the main. Course two-eighty.'

As *Lone Gull* with sheets eased picked up her skirts and ran with a far easier motion, carrying the sand-yellow seas along with her instead of bashing into them, Bill's eyes twinkled behind his glasses. 'This is what I like,' he cried jubilantly, 'a fair wind. And I suppose that if this wind did come on to blow

146

really hard we could run for it into the East Swale, couldn't we, skipper?'

Watching the point of the North Foreland cliffs dropping astern under our port quarter I recalled the unhappy end of a little yacht hereabouts many years before the war. Two impecunious young friends had bought a very ancient 6-ton cutter with a deep keel and a straight stem because she was so cheap, despite warning by experienced locals that the old girl was well known to be suffering from that weakening disease known as nail sickness. On their first cruise in her they were rounding the Foreland in very light airs, creeping in as close as they dared to the cliffs to miss as much as they could of the full run of a foul ebb tide. In the vicinity of an indent called Botany Bay their lead keel struck a flat ledge of rock that runs out from this point.

Their yacht grounded quietly enough and they at once laid off a kedge in the dinghy, but the tide was falling fast and ere long she was high and dry and lying far over on her bilge. The cheerful young owners were not unduly worried, for their little cutter was on a flat and quite smooth area of rock, the sea was calm, and they knew the next tide would be plenty high enough to float them. They accordingly resisted the offers from local longshoremen who hovered round with hungry eyes and expectant palms hoping to have the job of getting them off.

But when that evening the tide did make a slightly fresher breeze brought in a choppy sea, and as the cutter started to lift and drop back on the ledge her owners were horrified to see her planks open out and the sea well up inside her cabin. In a short time the lead keel had dropped off and the waterlogged hull began to fall to pieces, so that the two astonished mariners had to take to their dinghy with what possessions they could save from the wreck. Afterwards they told me that they had never imagined a yacht could break up so quickly – and the wreckage later showed that although on the whole the planking was hard and sound enough, for an old boat, all the fastenings had corroded away, and there was little left to hold the planking and frames together. This minor tragedy, for the unfortunate partners could not afford they said to have her insured, and they had no money to replace their loss, emphasized the fact that

147

however big and strong the frames and floors and planking of an old yacht might appear to be, a wooden vessel is only as strong as her fastenings.

'That'll be the Hook beacon, won't it, through the starboard rigging there?' Bill's voice broke in upon my reminiscence. 'Looks like a blown-out umbrella, doesn't it. I've never seen it before.'

The sands around the distant beacon with its inverted-cone topmark were already covered, but they were still giving us their shelter from the seas blown by the north-easterly wind, and *Lone Gull* was slipping along the coast in fine style. Over the low cliffs to port the twin towers of Reculvers broke the featureless Kentish skyline as we raced past the Hook Spit conical buoy.

'We'll keep well up to windward of the Horse Channel and West Last buoys,' I said looking over the chart, 'to allow for this strong west-going flood tide. It's about eight miles now to the Girdler lightvessel and I reckon we'll have to lay about oh-ten-oh, or say north by east, so as not to be swept down to leeward of it.'

The sea now had that brownish-green tinge peculiar to sand-laden estuary waters, with specks of white here and there as crests turned over. The seventeenth-century Dutch painters, the Van de Veldes father and son, knew exactly how to capture the colour and shape and movement, the very form of these sloppy estuary seas better than any of their contemporaries, although from amongst the English school of a later period I would say Charles Brooking (1723–1759) equalled their ability to record the current shipping scene and the water with uncanny integrity. In his short life of 36 years Brooking painted a large number of oils which showed many types of both Naval and merchant ships at their work with an accuracy of detail in hull and sails and rigging unsurpassed even by today's photography. In those days marine painters studied ships minutely until they understood the purpose of every piece of rigging, when and how it was worked, which ropes were taking a strain, which ones would be slack, and what the sea would look like under various wind conditions and sky effects. They trained themselves to *see* clearly. Many of today's artists, like new architects, cannot be bothered to make the necessary effort to study and learn about

148

the subjects they are trying to paint, and so we become dismally familiar with the blobs of bright paint representing ships, the splashes of colour to show impossible waves, the wild brush-marks to show a nightmarish coastline. Like some of the new architects' buildings, many of these works fall down when a wind blows and we think of the kind of sea that would assuredly be running.

Looking back over the water to where the tiny finger of the Hook beacon poked against the horizon I recalled vividly the last time I had been in these waters. It was not quite eight years before, in December of 1940, when we had been ordered with one of the specially equipped mine-recovery trawlers to proceed forthwith to Dover. Under cover of darkness and mist a German fast minelayer working fast for three nights had recently sown a large field of moored contact mines and protecting mine-sweep cutters just off the harbour, right under the noses of the Flag Officer in Command, Dover, and all his merry warships and crews. It was a brilliant piece of work and for the best part of a very dangerous mile it blocked the normal convoy channel through the Straits. Minesweepers in pairs with their Oropesa sweeps were out every day from dawn till dusk, but were re-porting sweeps lost through the ingenious explosive sweep-wire cutters with which the Germans had carefully surrounded every mine they had laid.

Nothing was known of the mines themselves – they could be horned contact, magnetic, acoustic, or even a mixture – and we had orders to work closely with the minesweepers, like a terrier following the hounds, to pick up and render safe any mines that were not detonated, open them up and send their interior mechanisms to the experts at Portsmouth to examine.

My veteran Lowestoft trawler, *Sailor King*, rolled her way from the convoy anchorage off Southend and headed for the North Foreland with a strong and bitter wind from the North dusting her port side with icicles. To avoid the long and exposed main ship lanes by way of the Knock John and Edinburgh Channels where the seas would be running high for a small wallowing trawler, I had the skipper take us through the old Four Fathom Channel and across the Kentish Flats to the Gore off Reculvers, in the opposite direction we were taking today in

Lone Gull, so as to gain some shelter from the outlying sands. With the flood tide on the make I knew there would be ample water for our 12 ft draught.

As darkness began to close in a heavy squall screamed out of the north and the wind increased to a full Force 8. Through flurries of snow we caught a fleeting glimpse of the Hook beacon a mile or so to windward, and already we were finding the seas smaller and less vicious as we worked in under the lee of the sands. Although the urgency of our mission had allowed us special permission to proceed on our way after dark, with recognition signals to flash should we be spotted by a friendly patrol vessel, or a trigger-happy shore battery and mistaken for an enemy vessel the more I thought of what conditions would be like round the North Foreland in pitch darkness and snow, and the passage through the Downs with no lighted buoys to pick up, the less I relished the idea. I decided to find if possible a snug anchorage where we could lie quiet and unseen until daylight.

'I don't like these roody shoals an' all, sir,' was the only comment from my weather-beaten, tough trawler skipper from Grimsby. 'Don't like 'em, I don't an' all!' I guessed he would be far happier facing this gale in the deeper waters of his peace-time fishing grounds.

Despite my skipper's misgivings, only too evident in his broad back and square head, I gave orders to steam slowly into the wind with the hand lead going. As soon as the leadsman's voice could be heard from the waist intoning 'By the maaark fower!' (he was a young barge hand in peace days, bless him and his kind) we stopped engines, let the ship drop back to give the anchor a satisfying sand-burying snub, and spent most of what was left of that long winter's night drinking mugs of thick trawlerman's tea while the windows of the wheelhouse froze up and the steel decks grew white with snow. We were snug enough with Margate Sand, now our friend, just to windward of us. And with daylight the wind became less vicious, and after giving the beacon a thank-you pull on the whistle cord for his night's shelter, we steamed on our way to report our arrival to FOI/C, Dover. Ten days later we were able to signal 'Mission completed' and head north again through the Downs to our Lowestoft base.

This time, however, the sky was clear and the sea calm and our only worry was the thought of marauding hostile aircraft in the area.

'Breezing up a bit, isn't it?' Bill was right. *Lone Gull* was roaring along with a slop or two appearing in the lee scuppers, and there was some white tracery work on the surface of the Estuary now. The wind was not only much stronger but colder, more penetrating. I clambered forward with the winch handle, and when we had four rolls in the mainsail and the jib lashed to the bowsprit out of harm's way, the old girl bustled along quite fast enough for these seas under reefed mainsail and staysail.

It was hereabouts on these cruel sands that I recollected another story I was told about a yacht called the *Daisybelle*, an old straight stem yawl of 16 tons or so, which had a nasty experience one dark night many years before. Her owner, then in his late seventies, told me the yarn one evening while we were sitting in the Royal Corinthian.

'We'd come across from Ostend, I and Pitt my skipper, and a lad we had with us, bound home to the Crouch,' he said. 'It was a fast passage with the wind coming sou'westerly. But as darkness closed in as we got abreast of the North Foreland and shaped our course up for the North East Spit the wind began to pipe up in earnest. We had to heave-to, drop the mizzen and get a reef in the main. By the time we were under way again it was pitch dark, and black as the inside of a cow but for the five flashes of the Foreland and the other lights along the coast. The ebb was already beginning to run to the north east'ard and I didn't like it one little bit, so I asked my skipper Pitt what he thought we ought to do. "Lay along the coost, sir," he said. He was a good Tollesbury man. "That'll blow hard afore dawn. We can find a lee along the coost, sir." So we hauled our sheets and just managed to lay along the South Channel with the lights of Margate, Westgate and then Birchington some distance to wind'ard of us. It was cold on deck, for the old *Daisybelle* hadn't any proper cockpit then, and I asked Pitt why we couldn't anchor just where we were until daylight. "Naw sir, we can't do that," he says. "Not yit anyways, sir. Nearer the Hook'll be the best place." So with that we carry on for another hour, wet and cold from the spray and the lights on shore getting farther and farther away all the time. "This'll do, sir" calls Pitt at last from the foredeck. "Come on, Ted, give us a hand with the jib." While the boy muzzled the flogging jib and lashed it down to the bowsprit, Pitt tried to let go the anchor. But there was some delay and a good deal of shouting and cussing from for'ard, and I gathered that boy had carelessly passed the jib lashing round the anchor stock in the dark. Pitt told him off right enough, but by the time the anchor was down and the mainsail stowed we seemed to be riding in a lot of white water. "She's draggin', that she is," said Pitt and started to veer more cable. But he'd no sooner done that than her heel came down on the hard sand with a bump that shook the rigging and almost knocked us off our feet, and it shook me, I can tell you. We managed to get the mainsail up again and Pitt and the lad began to heave in on the windlass, but they couldn't get the cable in, and in the end we had to give up, stow the main again, and just wait for next high water, while the bumping became less and she started to lie over. The *Daisybelle* was a deep boat, one of the old fashioned kind, and when the tide left us about midnight she lay so far over on her billage, as Pitt called it, we had to walk about on the cabin lining. It was altogether a wretched night, for the wind steadily veered more in to the west and blew even harder. It was as cold as charity out there on the sands in the pitch dark with the old boat on her side and the halyards thundering against both masts in the wind. And the roar of the seas breaking on the edge of the sands to wind'ard of us wasn't an encouraging sound in the dark, I can tell you. The hours dragged by very slowly as we sat on the edge of the settee in the saloon and the boy managed to coax mugs of hot cocoa off the galley fire. I laced mine with something stronger, and felt better for it, I can tell you. "What had we better do, Pitt," I asked, for I didn't like the look of things one bit. "Had we better light a flare for help?" But Pitt only shook his head. "Never you worry, sir," he said. "We'll have her afloat come daylight. And if we did signal for help, sir, it'd only call out them salvage men from Margate, and they're proper sharks, they are." I only hoped Pitt was right as we sat and waited until the water began to come back again. It was just beginning to get light in the East and still blowing hard from the west'ard when the old boat started to shudder with the waves hitting her. She lifted once or twice and fell back with a thud that shook her with a noise like thunder, and we had a job to hold on. Then as she lifted to another swell and fell back on to the hard sand once more the bilge water started to slosh up into the lockers behind the settees with a loud rushing noise. I found it unnerving enough, for I knew we drew nearly seven feet and I thought we'd have to wait some time before the water outside was deep enough to float us clear of the sand. I shall never forget as long as I live the sight of poor old Pitt's face as we fell with a heavier crash than ever and the water rushed into the lockers and squirted out into our faces through the ceiling ventilation holes. "Oh my gawd sir, wot 'as we done to deserve this," he cried. "*Her billage is acomin' in*, sir!" I've laughed about it since, but at the time I was as scared as he was, I can tell you. But we were nearly upright by now and that was the last time our lee bilge struck the sand before the old boat thudded several times with her heel and then at last rode clear on her anchor cable. Of course, as soon as the sharks in Margate caught sight of us in the daylight they were out and alongside in their yawls like a lot of vultures, but we were afloat now, although making a fair amount of water through an opened garboard seam, I think, and we kept them off with boathooks, the scoundrels, while we got underway again. And that evening as the wind went down at sunset we were in the Crouch again, safe and very glad, I can tell you, to pick up our mooring and arrange to have the old boat slipped next day. I've never been on the sands since that night, all the years I have been sailing, and never want another one like it!'

With the wind hauled just forward of our starboard beam *Lone Gull* was tramping through the short seas with a fine measured stride, sailing herself with a line around the tiller while Bill and I sat in the shelter of the cockpit munching sandwiches. It was cold enough today to have the cabin stove alight, and a small cloud of smoke blew away to leeward from the little chimney. 'What putrid weather for August,' Bill exclaimed. 'My goodness, I'm glad we came this way across the Estuary, skipper, and are not now bashing our way down the

Barrow Deep. Think what the East Swin would be like on the ebb!'

Slanting up to windward so that she could hold her own against the fierce lee-running tide *Lone Gull* surged handsomely past the red hull of the Mouse lightvessel until ere long the Blacktail Spit conical buoy with its topmark rising and falling on the edge of the Maplins was abeam and to windward of us. 'There's the first of the measured-mile beacons, and I think one of the withies marking the Broomway,' Bill said as he peered through the binoculars. 'But I'm hanged if I can see any entrance into Havengore, but you can see the bridge across the creek plain enough.'

'Never mind. The entrance will show up. How much water have we?'

He deftly swung the lead. 'Fathom and a quarter.'

The low line of the Essex shore was rapidly closing us, and the seas had lost their steepness and size, they were gentle now. From beneath our keel came a dull scraping sound.

'Board's touching,' I said. 'Better haul it up.'

Lone Gull's oak centreboard was easy to lift by hand, and even with it hauled right up with her ton of outside iron keel she would still tack and work to windward in smooth water, although naturally making more leeway. The noise and bustle of the sea was suddenly muted as the entrance to the creek uncannily revealed itself and our little ship swept in between the banks and another cast of the lead gave four feet. Although still blowing hard outside even the wind seemed here less boisterous, softer, appreciably warmer.

The bridge keeper had seen us and the great iron span was slowly lifted towards the sky as we rustled through the gap beneath. 'Where you from?' he hailed from his high perch on the bridge. When we told him he called back 'Ar, a bit dusty out there today, wasn't it?' We grinned back, thinking how very much more dusty and prolonged it would have been had we carried on with our original intention and threshed our way round by the Barrow Deep, the Swin and the long Whitaker Channel to the Rays'n and home. As it was because of our shallow draught we already were in smooth sheltered waters and could work our way through into the Roach, thence down

154

the Crouch and the Rays'n on the ebb that would shortly begin – if we felt energetic enough. But suddenly a feeling of great tiredness swept over me. We had made an excellent passage from Ramsgate and I felt I had had enough for one day.

'Let's bring up in Potton creek below Paglesham,' I suggested, 'and have a good meal.' Bill nodded and soon *Lone Gull* was lying with her wings folded, as snug as could be under the lee of the river wall. Seated in her cockpit with a drink in one hand I knew I no longer had the strength or stamina for too much of such boisterous cruising. One had to face the fact that, not only were we all several years older, but the long years of the war had done many of us, civilians and Service folk alike, what a smacksman friend liked to describe as 'a proper little bit o' *no good*'.

When the tide began to fall and the grass-covered bank to windward rose high against the quiet evening sky, the wind began to take off little by little and became soft and warm as new milk, whispering gently amongst the long grasses on the skyline. It was laden with the scents of the trees and meadows and dykes and wild flowers from the pasture levels of Potton Island. And as we watched from the cockpit the red sun sink over the mainland beyond Southend, Bill filled his curved pipe with a contented expression on his rugged face.

'Know one thing, Maurice?' he asked, puffing contentedly. 'I just wouldn't change places with anyone right now.'

Swan, 6 tons

14. *Designing mostly for comfort*

IN the calm of a warm evening when the wind has died after a breezy day, sitting as Bill and I were in Potton creek in the cockpit and doing nothing in particular except look around at the silent water and the saltings, saying very little, and that only in low voices so that the hush of nature should not be broken; this is a time of great contentment. And when the sun has hidden himself, the colours in the sky and on the surface of the water fade, and a chill comes in the air as darkness steals over the scene like a slowly closing door, the cabin of a small yacht offers the most welcoming warmth. For preference the cabin should be of a traditional kind with soft mellow woodwork in which the lovely grain of the panelling is reflected in the lamplight; and the light should be the warm glow of oil lamps, not the hard cold stare of tiny electric bulbs.

The settees should be wide enough with a soft cushion or two to invite one to recline at one end or the other. For me there would be no dinette, that arrangement of table on one side of the cabin with upright facing seats in the manner of a cramped British Rail 2nd-class dining car. Because someone had recently invented it I had given *Lone Gull* a dinette to starboard. For sitting up and eating meals in the day time it worked well enough, but for the hours of relaxation one can enjoy in a small boat's cabin after a hard sail it was not a success. Admittedly my galley was in its alcove formed by the centreboard case aft to port, and there was a full-length settee opposite the dinette, but only one person could relax fully on this settee, and any others on board who wanted to get their heads down had only the fo'c'sle berths or cushions in the cockpit for choice.

Yet the dinette arrangement has become a common feature of countless standard yachts produced in plywood or plastics. 'It converts to a double berth at night,' say the particulars glowingly, and the 6-ft long galley that takes up the whole of the opposite side of the cabin has been a godsend to the sleek salesmen at numerous boat shows: 'the wife always falls for that,' they tell you. When children are on board they can be kept safe from under parents' feet when sailing by being told to sit at the table, play their games, and not come out into the cockpit. At mealtimes with the children sitting at the table, knives and forks at the ready, poor perspiring Mum can stand at the super galley and deliver food to the ravenous mouths by merely turning round, like a devoted thrush at her nest. It is in fact not unlike the dining space advertised in the contemporary flat – a part of the kitchen with small check-clothed table and four upright chairs or two fixed seats with backs. The kids are used to it, and when at long day's end games are put away, sleepy little faces are tucked up and kissed good night in the fore-cabin, and Mum and Dad can at last clear the supper things in the sink and wash up, where do *they* relax for the remainder of the adults' evening? They can sit at the table as before and play cards, or rest their elbows so as to ease aching backs and look glassily into one another's faces; or they can go through the paraphernalia of dropping the table to fill the middle section of the double berth and arrange the cushions to cover it, and then what else is there to do but to make up the bed properly and turn in for the night? They can sit up with good books if the battery is well charged up and Dad doesn't mind both lights being on.

But with children in the crew life in a small cruising boat has to be a constant compromise, and for perhaps three-fifths of the time the dinette with big galley opposite layout undoubtedly does work well. For the new boating family days afloat are so exciting that it matters not a jot if the whole contemporary cabin does appear cold and clinical and somehow devoid of real comfort, for no one really has a chance to relax during the day.

For my choice I revel in a warmly lighted, comfortable cabin where three or four can recline with feet up at day's end. To complete the feeling of cosy warmth some form of heating stove is to me as essential as tight decks. In my experience the stove must burn solid fuel – smokeless coal, charcoal or even wood that you have beachcombed along the shore – if the whole cabin is not to drip with moisture as soon as the stove dies down.

157

Oil stoves and gas fires, while effective in giving a degree of
warmth, also create by their combustion a great deal of moisture
(in the case of the oil heater the quantity of moisture given off
is roughly equal to the amount of oil burnt) and a humid
atmosphere results, unless some form of flue through the deck
above for extracting the products of combustion is fitted. Small
slow combustion stoves suitable for yachts' cabins are available
through caravan supply stockists, and sometimes an old-
fashioned bogie stove, like the ones that heated countless air-raid
shelters during the war, can be found at a hardware merchants.
One of the joys of a coal stove aboard a yacht is to be able to
burn most of the rubbish instead of dropping it overboard in the
hope that it will sink, while on a passage it is pleasant to have a
big pot of coffee or a can of soup simmering quietly on the hob.

In the years that followed the war the yachting industry soon
began to reflect the growth of the Welfare State. More leisure
time given by the five-day week with longer weekends, and much
more money to spend on fun, resulted in thousands of people
taking to boating where formally there would be only hundreds.
Old ideas of the crippling cost of owning a yacht gave way to the
new idea that there could be a boat of some kind for everybody.
The first signs of a boom in boats became a flood, and possibly
for the first time in history there appeared to be a fair profit to
be made out of the yachting industry. Thinking that a fortune
could be made out of the boating craze new firms leapt on to
the bandwagon, many of them with no previous experience of
either boat building or of the tidal waters in which the boats
would be used. Some very unsuitable craft resulted, and many
firms eventually went bankrupt.

Books on yachting and boating for the beginner began to fill
the libraries. Through the keen sponsorship of Sir Max Aitken,
chairman of *Daily Express* Newspapers, the first of the post-war
annual international boat shows was organized by the Ship and
Boat Builders National Federation and held at Olympia in
London in January 1955. When three years later it moved to the
much larger building at Earl's Court this Boat Show became
the biggest exhibition of its kind in the world, and pleasure
boating started a boom in Great Britain that matched its
counterpart in the U.S.A.

At almost every show the launching of an entirely new boating journal was announced, and competition with the four long-established yachting magazines became steadily more intense. With the preparation of special Boat Show issues and show reports every year, the mid-winter break to sunshine for a week or two had to go by the board: the winter had now become the busiest time for all the yachting magazine staffs, and leave had to be in short spells when it could be seized during the summer.

The rapid growth of yacht building brought much new work to the architects, and I found myself caught in a spell of intense activity and worked over the drawing board most weekends. A natural development of the *Lone Gull* with a short sawn-off counter stern and 32 ft overall resulted in a centreboard version, *Carregwen*, being built at an Aberystwyth yard, and two keel versions of the same design, *Sixpence* and *Tinka* appearing at yards in Suffolk and Yorkshire. Like their elder cousin *Lone Gull* these boats proved to be good comfortable cruising yachts with an acceptable turn of speed, at least off the wind, for *Tinka*'s owner tuned her up to such an extent that one year she was winner of the points cup for handicap racing at Bridlington.

For many years I had admired the beautiful canoe-sterned yawls which had been produced during the first decades of the century by the artist-designer Albert Strange, a prominent member of the Humber Yawl Club. It occurred to me that a design for a pretty yawl could be developed with the Albert Strange model as a basis but with modern rig and interior lay-out. *Lone Gull* was ten years old and I had enjoyed some fine sailing in her, but the idea of experimenting with an entirely new design led me to sell her to an owner who for several years based her happily on Chichester Harbour where her shallow draught proved highly convenient. My new design was called *Tamaris* from the numerous tamarisk bushes that we could see on the bank from our moorings.

Tamaris had a canoe stern and a matching bow with what I thought was a sweet sheer, but unlike the old Strange yawls her deck amidships was raised. Instead of a coachroof, therefore, she had a large skylight and a low hatch so that the 8 ft pram dinghy could be carried bottom up beneath the mainboom. She

159

was built at Johnson and Jago's yard at Leigh, largely by
Jimmy Jago himself, a first-rate craftsman who not long after,
sad to relate, was found drowned in Bradwell creek, having
fallen overboard from his own yacht. Measuring 28·6 ft in
length, 24·0 ft on the waterline, 8·3 ft beam and 4·3 ft draught
with her fixed iron keel of two tons, *Tamaris* had both working
jib and staysail running on hanks on the stays. I still preferred
the divided headsail rig with the staysail working on a boom,
for Marjorie was unable to haul on sheets and halyards, and I
had to sail the boat virtually single-handed.

To obtain a useful area in the mizzen I brought the tiller up
into the cockpit from under the after deck and stepped the
mizzenmast over it, so that with the sternpost just aft of the
mizzen she was technically a ketch, but she was always referred
to as a yawl. *Tamaris* was a charming little boat, and because of
her large mizzen she would sail and tack easily in smooth water
under mizzen and one or both headsails only, while she would
do anything you liked under her mainsail alone. In course of
time she had a number of sisters built in various parts of the
world: one of them, *Triton* III, was based on Lake Lucerne
under the Swiss flag.

The old-time yawl, like my friend Jay's *Signora*, with a big
gaff mainsail and only a small leg-o'-mutton or lug mizzen with
its mast stepped on a thin counter-stern, had few advantages
over the traditional gaff cutter. Dropping the mizzen made little
difference to the sail area carried and was hardly equivalent to a
reef in the mainsail. Under the mizzen and forestaysail or jib
the old yawl would be very sluggish, and would hardly ever sail
to windward or come about in stays under this rig; the proportion of sail area in the mizzen compared with the rest of the
sail plan was far too small. In many yawls the most practical use
of the mizzen and its gear is to have shrouds for one to hold on
to when climbing aboard or when attending to the dinghy
painter on the after deck: mizzen shrouds were like today's
guard rails.

Yachting writers years ago used to advocate the value of a
yawl's mizzen in making her 'lie head to wind when riding out a
gale'. This has been shown countless times in practice to be only
wishful thinking, for the mizzen cannot fill on either tack,

160

however hard it is sheeted in, until the yacht is at least 4 points (45 degrees) off the wind, and then the strong wind pressure (and the seas) on the weather bow, bowsprit, mainmast and rigging forced her head off far more strongly than could be counteracted by the pressure of the wind in the mizzen. In a strong gale riding *ahull* (under bare poles, with no sail set) most yawls like cutters would take up their natural position relative to wind and waves, that is usually with the wind and seas just abaft the beam or on the quarter, whether the mizzen was set or not. And provided they were good, well-found yachts they usually came to no harm, for this has been shown to be the best method for conventional types of yacht to ride out extreme conditions of the order of Force 9 plus. The vessel must, however, have plenty of sea room to leeward to allow for drift, otherwise she may soon be in real trouble. In anything over Force 8 beating off a lee shore for a yacht much under 50 ft is usually out of the question, whatever her draught or type.

With the Bermudian sail plan of *Tamaris* I had aimed at getting a more balanced proportion of the canvas, and the mizzen having 30 per cent area of the mainsail was that much more effective. When the mizzen and jib were stowed she was perfectly balanced under the mainsail and staysail, and this proved her handiest sail plan in winds above Force 6. In any heavy weather it is a fallacy to rely on being able to continue comfortably under mizzen and jib, for a yawl's mizzenmast is rarely stepped firmly enough to stand the immense strain of gale winds, and it is always better under these conditions to keep the sail plan well within the ends of the ship.

Tamaris was a worthwhile experiment, for she showed me that a pretty little yawl could be made under modern rig to perform moderately well; but it was also clear that under most conditions handling and performance could (not necessarily would, but could) be better still under sail plan of a well-proportioned *ketch*, where the mizzen would have at least 50 per cent of the area of the mainsail and roughly equal that of the staysail. *Tamaris* eventually went to Northern Ireland to be registered at the Port of Belfast, where she has cruised, I am told, to the Baltic and other distant ports. Many people liked the look of *Tamaris* and her sisters, and based on her lines I was asked to

161

design two centreboard sloops which were to be built as sister-ships for two brothers and their families at the Leigh-on-Sea yard of Seacraft & Co. These boats, 27·5 ft overall with 8·4 ft beam and drawing only 3·0 ft with the wooden *Lone Gull* type centreboard hauled up, retained the raised midship deck of *Tamaris*, but with a large main hatch (it could be called a dog-house) to give standing headroom over the galley and after end of the cabin. The stern was of lifeboat or Scottish type with outboard hung rudder, as cost had to be considered and the true canoe stern of *Tamaris* with inboard rudder is difficult to build to look fair and is expensive.

These two boats, *Tringa* and *Cordelia*, served as family cruising boats for a number of years, and usually sailed at weekends with two or three children and a large dog amongst their crews, until all the children grew up and larger craft had to be obtained. These two double-enders led to orders for a number of other boats based on the same hull design, but with transom stern and lengthened to 29·0 ft overall, to be built at the same yard. The first of these larger craft had a centreboard like the *Tringa* class, but in the round dozen that followed the centreboard was omitted and shaped bilge keels fitted instead. They became the *Barcarole* class 8-tonners.

The notion that my ancient barge yacht *Swan* with her iron inboard leeboards had given me all those years before, the idea of having *fixed* leeboards or keels, had turned full circle. It was experimental at this stage, but we decided to fit bilge keels to these 29-footers composed of thick oak planks cut to a reasonably streamlined shape in plan and through bolted to heavy bilge stringers on the top of the boat's framing. These keels were fitted, in fact, in a similar manner to the traditional fin keel, and on many occasions when striking hard ground (once a rock off the Normandy coast) these boats proved how strong and well nigh immovable such bilge keels can be. I do not claim to be original in thinking of twin bilge keels for a cruising boat. At about the same time Mr Robert Tucker, one of Britain's most versatile and prolific designers of interesting yachts, had produced his design for the celebrated 17 ft Silhouette class chine boats, of which many hundreds were to be built in plywood and later in plastics and all with twin bilge keels, and he fitted twin bilge keels to numerous other designs as well. I was only experimenting with shaped wooden keels on traditional round-bilge carvel-built yachts of some size and weight.

The performance of these bilge-keel 8-tonners compared evenly, so far as we could judge, with the original centreboarder of this class. It was also pleasing to learn that when Mr Philip Hays, then a keen Flying Dutchman owner and racer, who took delivery of *Barcarole*, tried her out in the Thames Estuary off Whitstable, he found that the shoal-draught bilge-keel family boat would turn to windward, tacking without missing stays, in a smart breeze under her working jib only, with the mainsail stowed. Like the old-fashioned barge yacht these shallow-draught boats with their long straight ballast keels and short bilge keels proved themselves very handy indeed. Contrary to many peoples' belief the bilge keels appear to act like a barge's leeboards in helping the yacht to spin round in stays. With their ability to work into very shallow waters, like a centreboarder with her board up, and to sit upright on level ground and lie quietly on the mud at night while deeper yachts rolled their insides out, and the ease with which they could be hauled out and transported without the need for blocks and chocks, it looked as if the bilge keeler was to usher in a new era of cruising yachts.

Following the Barcarole series the next step was a somewhat larger design to be based on the same general type. This was a chunky version of a transom-sterned boat with the same midship-raised deck and the same sharp turn to the bilge and shallow draught of the Barcarole class, but 30·0 ft overall, 26·2 ft on the waterline, 9·5 ft beam, 3·3 ft draught and measuring just under 10 tons by Thames Measurement. The first two, named *Tidewater* and *Stealaway*, were built by Seacraft & Co for two friends who had them laid down side by side in the big shed on the Leigh foreshore where by now a dozen other bilge-keel yachts had already been constructed. These two were slightly non-standard, for as they were being built both owners decided to have the sterns drawn out a further 12 in. and the rudder stocks mounted that much inboard for the sake of neat appearance. It cost nearly £200 more to do this to each boat, showing that neat appearance can rarely be enjoyed for nothing! As one

163

of the owners was also well over 6 ft the main hatch was carried forward to the mast to give 6 ft 6 in. headroom below: this did not, in the designer's view, improve the yacht's appearance in any way, but it made a fine cabin.

Soon after being launched on to the hard beach the bilge keels of these boats were put to a rigorous test that justified the strength of their construction. They were sitting upright on the shore when a gale of wind from south-east blew up during the night. There was about a four-mile open fetch across the flats from the Grain shore on the Kent side of the Thames, and the sea that was running in had to be seen to be believed.

A number of yachts broke from their moorings on the South-end foreshore that day, and others started seams and damaged bilges on the ground. But although the two Tidewaters sisters like the other boats were lifted and dropped many times on the hard shore both on the flood and the ebb, neither showed any signs of damage nor were they apparently harmed in any way. The age-old method of fitting this type of fin keel by means of heavy bolts right through appeared to be fully justified.

The plans for this Tidewater class were drawn with the skilled amateur builder or the native yard with no experience of high-class yacht work in mind. Construction was as straightforward as I knew how to make it, with traditional stout carvel planking fastened with copper rivets (or rooves) to steam-bent timbers throughout, or it could be iron fastened to sawn frames of oak, jarrah, hickory, sapele or other local timber. In the next ten years sixteen of these Tidewater boats were to be built in English yards, as well as by amateur builders in back gardens in Australia, the West Indies and East Africa.

Various rigs were adopted amongst these boats, ranging from stemhead Bermuda sloop to Bermuda cutter with short plank bowsprit and a gaff cutter with traditional round bow spar; and they each gave some instructive data. For instance, these different rigs confirmed my own long-held belief that a beamy shoal draught boat of this type with very short overhangs forward and aft can rarely be made to balance satisfactorily under a stemhead sloop rig. For one thing, within the limited length between the stem and the transom it is impossible to get sufficient sail area to give the boat a fair sailing performance in

164

light weather. If you give her a much loftier mast to gain sail area upwards you will only cripple her, make her too tender to carry her canvas in normal fresh breezes; and if you lengthen the mainboom to gain the area in the mainsail (adding a bumkin at the stern to carry the masthead backstay clear of the boom end) then you find that she has too much sail aft of the mast to balance the stemhead foresail. She will then gripe so much that you won't be able to hold her, and it will make her very slow, for few things hold a yacht back so much as a large rudder blade constantly dragged through the water at an acute angle.

Whereas the slender racing yacht with 4 ft or 5 ft overhang at the bow and more aft can set well within her overall length all the sail area her lightly driven hull requires, and her racing crew can quickly change headsails as necessary and set enormous genoas, the chunky cruising boat cries out for more sail area forward of the mast, more headsails in fact. It was Dr Manfred Curry who in the 1920s in his book on *Yacht Racing Tactics and Sailing Aerodynamics* showed that on average in area for area a conventional yacht's jib or foresail could give 50 per cent more drive when close-hauled than her mainsail; which is to say that 100 sq. ft in a headsail can be expected to give the equivalent drive to windward to 150 sq. ft of mainsail. This theory has been confirmed by those Tidewater class boats which have had cutter rig, with an inner forestay and a topmast stay to a bowsprit about 5 ft long outboard. With working jib of about 110 sq. ft, set either on hanks on the topmast forestay or flying on a Wykeham Martin furling gear in addition to the forestaysail of some 120 sq. ft, the yacht carries only slight weatherhelm, and the improvement in sailing performance is improved beyond many owners' belief. But fashion in small yachts has always followed on the innovations of the racing classes, and it seems to be only the owners of greater experience who will recognize the advantage of a short bowsprit and two working headsails aboard a normal beamy cruising boat.

Another innovation so far as my own designs were concerned which I introduced with the Tidewater class was the fitting of shaped davits at the stern so that the dinghy could be carried slung up between them athwart the transom. This method of carrying the ship's boat at sea used to be common practice in Baltic ketches, New England traders and many other old-time ships. It is a convenient method of keeping the dinghy quiet and out of the way, but it limits the size of boat that can be carried to roughly the width of the stern, or at least 2 ft less in length than the yacht's beam.

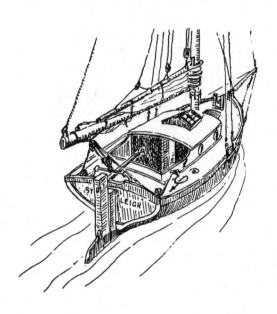

Storm, 7 tons

15. *Experiments and rigs*

IT has always been a cause of some regret to me that experimenting with yachts' rigs has to be so expensive. Putting fresh theories into practice in sails and their gear and equipment can be both fascinating, for the owner with an enquiring mind, and wholly instructive; but unless you confine yourself to sailing models you will need a bottomless purse and much patience. Over the years I had tried sailing my Bawley-type gaff cutter *Storm* as a sloop with a big headsail set on her bowsprit on a long wooden roller. It failed from weakness of the roller attachment to the winding spindle and other causes, and one learnt that without special and expensive gear there was a decided limit to this roller-blind type of headsail which worked perfectly in small racing boats. Then my attempts to design a really useful yawl rig for *Wild Lone* II, the 10-tonner I had built at Pin Mill, and later with the improved (*sic*) ketch/yawl *Tamaris* of 7 tons, built for me at Leigh-on-Sea, were at least instructive and enabled me to visualize a better proportion of mizzen and mainsail areas in relation to displacement. I should like to have pursued these ideas and produced for experiment an almost perfectly balanced Bermuda ketch, but neither funds nor available time would run to it. A series of model yacht tests might have been the answer.

There is no doubt that the original Bembridge Redwing class of one-design racers, produced first I believe by the late Charles E. Nicholson in about 1897, assisted in the development of contemporary racing rigs more than any other single class. The Bembridge Sailing Club had a far-seeing rule that although the boats were all of a one design and in theory were identical, they were permitted to race under any rig they chose with the proviso only that the total rig must not exceed 200 sq. ft in area. At first the current rig was a large gaff or gunter-lug mainsail and small foresail, but as there were owners in this class with curious ideas and ample funds the Redwings over the years showed some hair-raising innovations. Early on a form of Bermudian mainsail was tried, but mast tracks had not yet been invented, its gear like the true rig of the Bermudas was clumsy, and it showed no superiority over the contemporary sloops in the class. There appeared an umbrella sail socketed to a short mast, but this neither took off nor took home any trophy. Leg-o'-mutton sails, fully battened sails, Chinese junk sails, even the Ljungström divided mainsail in turn put in fleeting appearances, but the results were always the same: each innovation showed some advantage over all the others on one particular point of sailing, but over a racing course each failed to beat the conventional rig of the day, whatever it was. Now experimenting in even a small one-design class has become prohibitively expensive, but it is some compensation for contemporary yachtsmen to know that many ingenious minds are busy with experimental work on new sailing-hull forms and rigs, aerodynamics and hydrodynamics amongst the members of the very active Amateur Yacht Research Society, at Woodacres, Hythe, Kent, England, whose instructive bulletins are available to the public.

Some years before the war I became interested in the possibilities for ease of handling offered by the *wishbone rig*. This was essentially a normal Bermudian ketch, but instead of a main sail between the masts a big staysail was set within the two halves of a divided spar, in shape like a narrow wishbone which was kept aloft pivoted to the mainmast and sheeted to the mizzen masthead. It was being developed in the USA by Frederic A. Fenger, a naval architect with whom I had a long discussion when visiting his country for the America's Cup races in 1937; while in this country Uffa Fox had incorporated this rig in his design of *Wishbone*, a handsome 83 ft fast cruising yacht built by Samuel White at Cowes in 1935 (see *Uffa Fox's Second Book*, Peter Davies, London, 1935). One day Sir Frederick Browning told me that the ancient 32 ft ex-Porthleven lugger owned by himself and Lady Browning (Daphne du Maurier, the novelist) needed all new sails; they wanted to toy with this wishbone rig aboard her, and what did I think about designing the rig for her. It seemed to be a fine opportunity to put theory into practice, and the result was that next season the Brownings' dark-blue-hulled ex-lugger *Restless of Plyn* sprouted a smart wishbone ketch rig with all tanned sails on her two white-painted masts.

On a fine weekend sailing out of Fowey with the owners I was agreeably surprised to find how light and easy it was to set and furl all the comparatively small sails, all of which ran either on a track or on hanks on stays, and sailing *Restless* with her wheel steering seemed child's play after the heavy West-Country fisherman rig. But in light airs aft the impression persisted that the deep old hooker needed a greater area of canvas, and one puzzled how to give her more off the wind with this engaging rig. With wind abeam or when close-hauled and plenty of it *Restless* showed how fast she could go in the long Channel swell, and how handy even a boat of this type could be under a versatile rig.

After the war General Browning, who was then Controller of Prince Philip's household in London, commissioned me to design for his family a canoe-sterned 40 ft ketch with something under 10 ft beam and 6·6 ft draught to replace the old hooker which had not survived the war years. The new boat was to be wishbone rigged with the benefit of the experience we had with the pre-war attempt. Named *Jeanne d'Arc* the new boat was built of first-class materials by good craftsmen at the small shipyard opposite Fowey which the Brownings had acquired, the same shipyard that had figured largely in Daphne du Maurier's early novel, *The Loving Spirit*.

For many years *Jeanne d'Arc*'s colourful hull and striking rig became a part of local regattas, for Boy Browning as his friends knew him was an enthusiastic sailor and got the best out of the little ship he loved. The rig, like that of the old *Restless*, was a joy to set and work, but it had its tribulations as we found by trial and error. The first wishbone spars, of spruce, were too heavy and gybing caused severe shocks through the sheet to the mizzen head. A second pair, specially made of light alloy to drawings, proved unable to bear the strain and buckled in a Force 7 breeze one day off Dodman Head. What with the wishbones and the various items of ironwork that had to be specially made the whole rig became very expensive and I was relieved that I did not have to foot the bills.

169

One irritating feature which we tried unsuccessfully to over-come was the habit of the wishbone to gybe monotonously, flopping back and forth when there was a light wind aft and *Jeanne d'Arc* rolled as all deep-draught yachts of modest beam tend to do. We put a substantial coil spring in the standing end of the wishbone sheet but despite this the mizzen masthead was subjected to rhythmic shocks as the spar fell from side to side and twanged its sheet. Only by sheeting the spar in as hard as we could to the mizzen mast could we keep it quiet, but then the biggest sail in the ship, the wishbone staysail, was nearly fore and aft and lost all its drive down wind.

This constant gybing showed us another, and far graver, weakness of the rig: namely, the danger of the sheet parting. Should this happen the wishbone spar is free to swing from side to side to its full extent, and if the wire sheet is still attached it will behave like a lash in the hands of an angry stockman. This is, I understand, precisely what happened one blustery and pitch dark night aboard the unhappy 83 ft *Wishbone*. The sheet parted near its lower end, and as the divided spar took charge aloft and thrashed back and forth the wire sheet continually zipped through the air slicing within reach of the brave but helpless hands on deck. They got the gear under control somehow, but it must have been an unpleasant experience. After we had been eight seasons sailing and testing *Jeanne d'Arc*'s sail plan she shed her wishbone and reappeared next year under a normal Bermuda ketch rig which I had designed for her owner. I believe she still sails as a conventional ketch and is, by and large, happier for it.

My hobby of experimenting with different designs of yachts which made me ready to change my own boat every few years was matched in my wife by a readiness to move house and home. Marjorie had a gift for seeing what could be done to transform an unpromising looking property into an attractive and welcom-ing home, whereas many viewers could see nothing but a dull and far from enticing house surrounded by a neglected garden. No doubt through having inherited my mother's restless temperament I have seldom been averse to change of environ-ment: indeed there is nothing I enjoy so much as travel, preferably by sea or train, and had I not had to meet the exacting schedule of an editor's life I should probably have

170

wandered over most of the world. With Marjorie's flair for home-making, therefore, it is not to be wondered at that we lived in and moved from half a dozen houses before I retired from the London rat race.

Moving house every few years became for us something of a well organized military operation, while we seized each opportunity to rid ourselves of the surplus domestic rubbish all households accumulate over the years and to collect pieces of attractive furniture. We must have been heaven-sent clients for estate agents and solicitors and removals firms; these cheerful guys got to know some of the Griffiths pieces well. 'Knob come off in me 'and last time,' one of them would grin, 'didn't it guv'nor?' Nevertheless, we began to learn a great deal about properties. We became familiar with rising damp and different kinds of damp-proof course, with a spreading roof, with settlement cracks, faulty guttering, blocked drains, smoky chimneys, warped doors, leaky taps, noisy cisterns; and of course with gardens that needed pulling round, as it is called, at the cost of aching muscles and a neglected boat on her moorings. But our knowledge and experience expanded, and we became expert in modern plumbing, in knocking down walls, in putting extensions on to rooms, and in various types of central heating. To me it was like surveying and buying and selling yachts all over again, and we felt we could ourselves become property surveyors.

While Marjorie, with her flair for redesigning rooms and her eye for attractive colour schemes and furniture arrangements, completely transformed one ordinary property after another into what our estate agent friends glowingly termed a highly desirable residence, my early training in the estate office at Ipswich came back to me. Marjorie's enthusiasm for houses and what some imagination could do to them was infectious, and with the useless and irritating hindsight of which we are all capable at times I sometimes wished I had forsaken the tyranny of the office desk soon after the war, and launched us into the property market. Whether that would have led us to wealth and long holidays in the sun and happiness, or merely to endless work, worry and little profit, only the gods would tell. As it was we did our best to solve the old problem of a satisfactory compromise for the daily breadwinner between a place within

171

tolerable distance for commuting to London by train and within easy weekend reach by car of our boat's mooring. Seven years – a long stretch for us then – in a charming little coach house in Haslemere, which we almost doubled in size before we sold it and moved to a flat in London and a house in Suffolk, only confirmed the fact that too long a daily journey would eventually wear down an ageing man.

The effects of the annual Boat Shows in London amongst the hundreds of thousands who visited them were beginning to show throughout the yachting industry. The advent during the war of plywood of a quality suitable for boat hulls had introduced the amateur builder to a material which would cut out much of the laborious and skilful work of framing up a hull and then covering it with dozens of separate planks, each with seams that could leak. With sheets of marineply the home boat builder found that he could cover a boat having straight sides and a V-bottom as if he were papering a wall – almost. Plywood now made it possible for thousands of handymen to build V-bottoms or chine hulls; it also made it easy for numerous new boat yards, which employed only unskilled labour, to produce them in large numbers – in some cases with regrettable results.

A wave of home boat building, never seen before in this country, was inevitable, and designers of small craft were quick to produce designs of simple boats specially for unskilled amateurs to build. For some years, in addition to a technical advice service the *Yachting Monthly* had been offering its readers, sets of plans were available to amateur builders for a purely nominal few guineas. Whilst these designs, ranging from a 13 ft half-decked dinghy to a 20 ft centreboard, round-bilge sloop, proved popular and numbers of small craft were built to them, readers' letters indicated an ever-increasing demand for something larger, a boat in fact that was:

1. Simple for the amateur to build and planked with plywood.
2. A good enough seaboat for, say, estuary cruising.
3. Safe (non-capsizable) in squally weather.
4. Large enough for mum and dad and one (perhaps two) children to sail in and sleep on board.
5. Not too large for one man to build in his garden or shed.

6. Able to be lifted on to road trailer and transported home for the winter lay-up.

Boiled down to essentials these appeared to be the needs of a very large number of up-and-coming yachting families, and in the office we had long discussions and made many sketches with much rubbing out before a plan emerged. The lines that finally appeared on my drawing board were for a chine boat with raised topsides, 24 ft in length, with a generous beam of 8 ft, a central cast-iron ballast keel to ensure self-righting qualities, and twin bilge keels of mild steel flanged plates so that the boat would sit upright on level ground or on a trailer. The rudder, mounted inboard of the rounded transom stern, was fully protected from striking the ground by a steel plate skeg, and the draught of the boat when floating upright was only some 2 ft 2 in. Kenneth Gibbs, yacht builder and designer with his own yard at Shepperton-on-Thames, who had long helped us to wrestle with the growing readers' technical advisory service, gave valuable advice and assistance in details of construction and planning. It was known as the *Yachting Monthly* 24-ft *Eventide*.

One of the first sets of plans was sent out to a Lieut.-Commander (E) Edward Atkinson who was then in Singapore. Some time later we received a letter from him telling us that he was getting on well with the building of the boat, and that as he was shortly due to retire from Naval service he had decided to sail back in her to his home at Emsworth, Hants. In view of this, he asked, did we recommend him to make any alterations to the plans or any special strengthening of the hull. It was a good question, and we rechecked the plans carefully. But the Y.M. Eventide had been designed from the first as a stiff little cruising boat to be safe at sea, and with her iron ballast keel and steel bilge keels she was intended to withstand all the rough and tumble of coastal and estuary cruising which would sooner or later entail grounding heavily on the hard sands without unduly damaging herself. We replied, therefore, that in our opinion Atkinson's Eventide needed no additional strengthening of either hull or gear to be fit for such a voyage.

Borer Bee, as she was called after the voracious insect that Atkinson said was eating into the timber almost as fast as they could build the boat, with sail number YME8 was accordingly completed exactly to the plans. With Fred Fisher, a 23-year-old ex-Naval rating as his crew throughout the voyage, and an outboard motor as sole auxiliary power for calms, Atkinson left Singapore in February 1959 and fetched up off Emsworth in October. Needless to say, the 8,000-mile voyage was not without incident. While turning to windward up the Red Sea *Borer Bee* was carried on to a coral reef. She was lifted by the swell and dropped heavily several times on to her port bilge keel before she was able to work off into deep water again. In an account of his voyage which Atkinson wrote in the *Yachting Monthly* (in January and February 1960) he had this to say of this incident:

'I thought the bilge keel would be bent or wrenched off [but] another swell and we were over the reef and in deep water again, sailing offshore on the port tack. A big advantage of bilge keels had been demonstrated. Without them the planking would surely have been badly damaged if not holed, and the ship would possibly have become a total loss. Later examination of the bottom revealed no signs of the grounding on the bilge keel plate and no movement whatever to the bottom stringer through which the bilge keel is bolted.'

From Port Said all the way to Malta, a distance of roughly 1,000 miles as the crow flies, *Borer Bee* found nothing but head winds to beat against. Sometimes it blew hard as Atkinson described in his account of this part of the voyage:

'Daylight on the 28th [June] brought with it a strong westerly wind which waited until we had finished breakfast before gusting to Force 7 and tearing our large foresail. It blew hard all night and at 0320 we shipped a large green one over the head. The man on deck hove-to, pumped out, reefed and got underway again without waking the watch below. It says much for the seaworthiness of *Borer Bee* that events such as these are rare enough to warrant mention.

'The next two days saw us tacking along the African coast. On 2 July the large foresail started to tear, but we got it down just in time. In the dog watches, being very tired, we decided to

174

heave-to for the night. After reefing the main and backing the storm foresail we cooked ourselves an excellent supper and washed it down with a bottle of Egyptian red wine and turned in. Next morning bright and early I went into the cockpit feeling much refreshed. It was a wild looking morning, blowing hard, but *Borer Bee* was lying very snugly on the wind. Then I felt a few drops of rain. It was the first we had had since leaving the Malacca Straits and my first reaction was to tear off my clothes and grab a piece of soap. Since then I have learnt the motto "trysails before trousers". Suddenly a terrific gust hit us and *Borer Bee* lay right over on her beam ends. Fred was through the hatch like a Jack-in-the-box, but before we could do anything the mainsail had degenerated into three white flags flapping wildly from the luffrope in a token of surrender to the elements. As we gathered in the remains the waves increased in height and started breaking.

'We lay a-hull under bare poles, but soon the sea conditions became very bad indeed and we were frequently caught in broken water. When this happened *Borer Bee* would move rapidly sidewards to leeward with the wave, and water would pour over the weather side into the non-self-emptying cockpit. I am quite sure that, had our 2 ft 6 in. draught been a foot or two greater, the lateral resistance of the keel down in the unbroken water, acting like a drogue underneath the boat, would have resisted this movement, and much more water would have been shipped.

'In the middle of pumping operations the bilge pump got blocked and had to be stripped; but even during this operation the bilge water never rose to more than an inch above the cabin sole. Throughout the forenoon we sustained several direct hits, but in the afternoon, though the general situation did not look much better, we encountered no more breakers, though there were several near-misses. Next morning with the wind northwest Force 5 we set the trysail and storm jib and resumed our beat to windward along the African coast.'

For a 24 ft plywood sloop designed for amateur construction the Eventide had fully justified its modest claim to be a safe little seaboat, and the design soon became the most popular of

175

the *Yachting Monthly* series. In the next few years over five hundred of these boats were to be built in back gardens, in garages and in various yacht-building yards all over the country, while others appeared in back yards in many parts of the world.

Very soon readers began to ask for plans of a larger version, and suggestions ranged in every size from 26 ft up to 36 ft in length. So many variations would not be practicable, but before long the plans of a 26 ft version were produced, and the extra 2 ft of length permitted less crowding with full-sized berths for four adults, galley, oilskin locker and lavatory compartment. The increased length and weight – for the ballast keel was heavier – made for a slightly faster boat better able to punch into a short head sea. Many of these 26 ft Eventides were built and some made the long haul across the Indian Ocean from Australia and New Zealand to Durban on their way across to the West Indies or northward to the Mediterranean. Enterprising owners in various parts of the world produced their own enlarged versions of this design with the necessary adjustments to ballast keel weight, sail and rigging plan, and details of construction, and there are backyard-built Y.M. Eventides which have emerged on to the waterfront as 27, 28 and 30-footers with a variety of individual layouts. In few things can a man show his own individuality so readily as in his boat.

For many years few, if any, new barge yachts had been built. The type, since the death of E. B. Tredwen, had been neglected by builders and yacht designers who had turned their attention more towards the merits of twin bilge keel craft. An exception was one picturesque miniature Thames barge complete with spritsail rig which was 35 ft in length, 11·2 ft beam and 2 ft draught, called *Tiny Mite*, which was built by J. W. Shuttle-wood at Paglesham in 1956. Yet the miniature barge yacht still offered advantages for owners in the Estuary and elsewhere who were forced to keep their boats on half-tide moorings, and needed a minimal draught, and amongst the requests we received for plans of a bigger Eventide were a number for a real barge yacht with leeboards, designed to be equally practicable for the amateur to build.

You cannot satisfy everyone with any single design, but we decided to find out if it was possible to meet the greater number of these requests with one set of build-yourself plans. Recalling the measurements and general proportions of the old Tredwen barge *Curlew* (remember 'Barney's Barge'?), for the sake of the minority who wanted a barge I worked out on my drawing board at home a 30-footer with 26 ft waterline length, 8·5 ft beam at deck and a draught with leeboards raised of two feet. This boat had more freeboard and headroom in the cabin than old *Curlew*, a more pronounced rise to the bottom, and with an outside iron keel of some 1,200 lb weight and inside ballast she was designed to be self-righting should she be laid flat on her beam ends at any time. A partially-balanced rudder of the same type as we had introduced in the Y.M. Eventide protected by a substantial skeg was also included. At the same time, to meet the requests of the majority the sets of plans included a bilge keel version of this boat in which the hull was identical from the deck down to the garboards, but had a deeper iron keel of some 3,300 lb weight and steel plate bilge keels giving a draught of 3 ft.

These boats were to be specially strongly constructed to withstand the wracking strains of constantly grounding at moorings or once in a while on outlying sandbanks in the Estuary. The planking could be either $\frac{5}{8}$ in. marineply or normal 1 in. carvel or strip planking fastened to framing regularly spaced throughout from stem to stern. The roomy interior in this form of hull offered scope for a variety of accommodation layouts with four, five or six berths. Named the *Yachting Monthly Waterwitch* the bilge keel version with 3 ft draught was classed the Mk I, and the barge version with 2 ft draught the Mk II. The plans were announced and published in the issue for May 1961.

As it was essentially a barge with maximum accommodation within a 30 ft length and intended for construction by the unskilled owner, it was impossible for us to disguise the boxy and angular appearance of the *Waterwitch*. 'A sailing caravan' was not an inappropriate or infrequent description, but the design appeared to meet the needs of many sailing families, and in the next few years a large number of these boats were built by different yacht yards or in back gardens in the United Kingdom and over the world. And whether they were Mk I or Mk II

177

versions, these boxes showed that they really could sail to everyone's satisfaction, and they could turn to windward in and out of narrow creeks in a very handy manner.

That the *Waterwitch* could also put up with any amount of rough weather off shore was proved over and over by some of the blue water voyages made by these yachts. Perhaps the most impressive were the cruises made by *Iota*, a Mk II version with leeboards. Built by her owner, S. A. Simpson, at his home in Sydney, New South Wales, the *Iota* was shipped one year to Tahiti, from whence she cruised around the Society Islands for two months, encountering some strong winds when she had to run under bare poles trailing warps, before being shipped back home to Sydney. The next year, starting from Mackay, South Queensland, she cruised along the Great Barrier Reef as far as Green Island in North Queensland and back. A second time *Iota* went out to Tahiti and explored the Marquesas islands in very mixed weather. The owner's stories of all three two-month cruises were published in the *Yachting Monthly* in January and February 1963 ('This Dream came True'), April 1964 ('In the Wake of Cap'n Cook') and in March and April 1966 ('*Iota* returns to the Pacific'). In more recent years *Iota* has cruised around the Caribbean and the West Indies.

Asked on one of his visits to the Y.M. offices in London, Mr Simpson told us that he selected the Y.M. Waterwitch design to build as he had for years cruised in a conventional 50 ft ketch and found out the limitations of her 7 ft draught for exploring out-of-the-way places, which he longed to do. He decided he would need a *portable* boat which could be shipped to the Pacific islands and explore from the base. He chose the Mk II leeboard version with 2 ft draught because, as he said, there are many lagoons in the Pacific with so little depth that a draught of even 3 ft can be just a little too much to get into them.

Contemplating some of these ocean voyages made by boats of both the Waterwitch and Eventide classes, it is gratifying to think of the numerous families who are afloat every year and enjoying these little ships, and to think also how so many of them have shown how safe and inherently seaworthy even a homely box, a floating caravan, can be at sea!

16. *Bilge keels and centreboards*

HAVING been without a boat of my own for three years I began to think that I might plan a new ship based on my pre-war *Lone Gull* as a traditional transom-stern shoal-draught type, but modified to benefit from current thinking. For my purpose *Lone Gull* had been a highly satisfactory boat of her kind and I always remembered her with affection for the way she had fulfilled all my simple needs in cruising around the coast and exploring shallow creeks. Now that the costs of building in similar style had risen between five and six times what they had been when I built her in 1938, the new ship just had to be somewhat smaller and trimmed in certain details to reduce costs if I was going to afford to build again at all.

The result was *Lone Gull* II, a fairly conventional carvel-built shallow-draught cruising boat with short overhangs like her predecessor but with stemhead sloop rig, an iron ballast keel of just under 2 tons, and in place of a centreboard, two shaped oak bilge keels. Whereas *Lone Gull* had been 10 tons by Thames Measurement, the new boat worked out at 8 tons. She measured 28·0 ft in length, 24·0 ft on the waterline, 9·0 ft beam and drew 3·3 ft in cruising trim. A working sail area of 248 sq. ft in the mainsail and 150 sq. ft in the jib proved adequate for the designed displacement of 11,500 lb., and with an air-cooled twin-cylinder hand-starting Lister diesel of $8\frac{1}{2}$ rated horse power she had a cruising speed of 5·5 knots with a maximum under power of 6·25 knots. The same raised midship deck arrangement as used in the *Tringa, Sixpence, Barcarole, Tidewater* and *Tamaris* class boats, having a short well deck forward and a substantial 5 in. high rail abaft the after break round the stern, gave *Lone Gull* II an especially roomy cabin with standing headroom under the beams and 6 ft 5 in. under the raised mainhatch. The well-tried accommodation layout with two full-size berths in the forecabin, a lobby with sliding doors and lavatory and washbasin to starboard with a large dry clothes hanging locker opposite, saloon with two 6 ft 6 in. berths, galley aft to port and chart table and oilskin hanging locker to starboard, was found very satisfactory, and emphasized in its roominess by the 3 ft 4 in. wide cabin floor.

As Marjorie and I were then living in our coach house at Haslemere, the boat was built for us at the yard of Harry Feltham. This yard is in a fascinating part of Old Portsmouth close to the inner harbour, the Camber, which can be seen of much the same size and shape as it is today in a map of the town dated 1595. At that date Her Majesty's Dockyard, begun during the reign of Henry VIII, was already building and refitting Queen Elizabeth's ships, which were of considerable size. And from Alf Pearce. an old ex-Navy man, we were able to rent a convenient mooring at Hardway on the west side of the Harbour and leave *Lone Gull* II in Alf's good keeping.

For two years, limited generally to odd weekends and a week's holiday for cruising, we thoroughly enjoyed sailing in the clear and colourful waters of the Solent and the Wight once again. Using her shallow draught and ability to sit upright with her bilge keels *Lone Gull* proved over and over how useful such a boat can be in working her way into the less crowded parts of the Solent rivers and creeks and rithes. On the tide we explored Bembridge, in Fishbourne creek we carried on nearly up to Wootton bridge and settled on the mud for the night away from the jam of deep-keel yachts that crowded together in the only part of the creek where they could lie afloat; and in Newtown River we again escaped the congestion by seeking a berth well above the rest with our keels on the mud at low water. On Saturday afternoons we found it essential, if one was to find a berth for the night at all, to hurry into places like Cowes, Newtown, Lymington or Keyhaven early in the afternoon, so crowded was every place. By 1500 hours the pierhead at Yarmouth would carry the notice HARBOUR FULL.

The effects of the boating explosion, successive boat shows and an enthusiastic yachting press, were showing themselves in no uncertain manner; and fine as it certainly was for thousands of boating families, this crowding was not what I aimed for when I escaped from London and went afloat in my little ship.

180

But with the aid of Adlard Coles's very excellent *Creeks and Harbours of the Solent* and the trusty leadline we explored all the less-known places we had time to discover in Solent waters, and from Chichester Harbour with its fingerlike pattern of creeks in the east to Poole Harbour and its lakes and river up to Wareham in the west, *Lone Gull* brought her shallow-draught and bilge keels and used them both to our great contentment.

She brought me satisfaction in proving to be a docile little boat to handle under almost all conditions, and friends who were sceptical about bilge keels and came to sail with us remarked with surprise how well she went to windward and how light on the helm she seemed to be. Like the Y.M. *Waterwitch* and *Eventide* this boat had a rudder blade of generous area with a small part of it forward of the pivot line giving it a certain amount of balance. This type of semi-balanced rudder had proved its value in boats of very shallow draught when they were sailing with the sand only a few inches beneath the keel, when many yachts begin to lose control. Any weight on the rudder when sailing is automatically reduced, and aboard *Lone Gull* in a breeze up to Force 6 you could steer her with one hand without straining, and with two fingers only in lighter breezes.

The bilge keels undoubtedly act as roll-damping fins. Although in all my centreboard and bilge-keel designs I have aimed to produce sections that in themselves will not encourage excessive rolling, *Lone Gull* was even less inclined to roll, either when at anchor or when running down wind. With a sea running up from aft or on either quarter she would give two quick rolls as the sea passed under her, and immediately settle back on course without any more rolling, almost as if she were running on a track. There was never any of that sick-making pendulum motion that so many yachts with slack midsections, deep draught and heavy-ballast keels set up, the abominable and sometimes dangerous rhythmic rolling.

A friend of mine made two crossings of the Atlantic from Falmouth to the West Indies. On the first occasion he sailed in a fine old-fashioned cutter of traditional English narrow and deep type, and told me that running down the Trades for three weeks on end she rolled every three to four seconds, dipping her rails each side over and over again, until the crew were almost

181

exhausted. Yet on a wind she sliced through the seas like the thoroughbred she was, and was always very fast.

A few years later he made much the same passage, this time from Southampton to Barbados, in a Hilliard 40 ft ketch, a V-bottom chine type with a modest draught just over 4 ft. He told me afterwards that this boat, to his surprise, ran straight with less tendency to bore her head and gripe than the old cutter had shown, and she hardly rolled at all. The flat sections of the V-bottom evidently acted as dampers, while there was no pendulum-like lead keel deep down to start the motion of rolling.

In spite of her long straight keel, *Lone Gull* never once missed stays while I had her. Normally in going about you pushed the tiller steadily but slowly to leeward, eased the jib sheet, left the tiller as she continued round in a sweep, and hauled in the other jib sheet as she settled on her new tack. Should there be the need, you could also box her round smartly by pushing the tiller hard down, and she would come round very quickly. As in the barge which can turn quickly pivoting on her leeboards, *Lone Gull* would appear to pivot on her short bilge keels, much as her predecessor would pivot on her centreboard. The bilge keels, far from making a yacht sluggish in stays as is thought by the sceptical, tend to make a yacht handier. Several other yachts have since been built to this *Lone Gull* II design, and I have discussed the way they handle with their owners, and every one appears to handle much as my boat did. She was evidently not a freak, but good balance on the helm, handiness in stays, and ability to stay on course unattended with tiller pegged or held with shockcord, appeared to be inherent in the design.

*

What really are the joys and snags of having a yacht with twin bilge keels compared, say, with those of a centreboarder? They might be enumerated in this way:

TWIN BILGE KEELS

Advantages

1. Shallow draught enables a yacht to work into rivers with

sand or shingle bars, and into small harbours that dry out at low water, and to use the shallower parts of anchorages where deep keel yachts cannot lie afloat.

2. If you do run aground, or decide to spend the night on the mud, your boat will generally sit squarely upright if the ground is level.

3. Putting the boat ashore for examination or a scrub is simple and calls for no legs or post or quay to lean against.

4. Hauling out on a slipway or on-to a road trailer is simplified as the bilge keels act as built-in shores and chocks.

5. Bilge keels act as roll damping fins and steady a boat's motion at sea.

6. When a yacht is sailing close-hauled and heeled say 15–20 degrees, the bilge keel to leeward becomes almost upright, increasing the effective draught by several inches and thereby reaching its most effective angle for reducing leeway.

7. The fitting of twin bilge keels calls for strong construction, which can ensure a tight hull, and it causes no obstructions in the cabin.

Disadvantages

1. When lying against a strange harbour wall or quay on the ebb any underwater ledge or sloping causeway must be watched in case the inside bilge keel gets hung up on it.

2. If you run aground on the ebb in light weather with the yacht sailing almost upright, you will not be able to reduce her draught by heeling (careening) her as you could with a normal single-keel yacht.

3. On the hard when scrubbing or antifouling the bottom, it is sometimes difficult to reach inside the bilge keels and underneath the hull here.

4. If on the ebb your yacht grounds on a steep-to shoal, such as a mussel bank, and cannot get off, you will not be able to make her list in towards the bank as you can a single-keel yacht, and she will settle at the angle of the ground. This may be inconvenient, but not dangerous, but should the bank be very steep indeed and your boat in danger of burying her lower bilge keel into the mud and lying so far outward as to risk filling when the tide returns, it may be necessary to lay out the

kedge anchor on to the bank (well buried) with a line to the masthead hauled taut.

5. When close-hauled in light airs and baffling head winds any yacht of very light draught with no drop keel is at a disadvantage and makes excessive leeway, and a bilge-keel yacht is no exception. At a speed through the water of less than one knot the poor aspect ratio of the bilge keels (the length of leading or biting edge to the overall length of the keel) can cause the bilge keels to stall, as a plane does if it loses its critical air speed. When this occurs the effectiveness of the bilge keels to hold the yacht up to windward falls away, and she will start sidling to leeward like any other very shallow-draught vessel. Under these conditions nothing is effective but a *deep keel*, or a drop keel such as a large centreboard, which will present a longer leading edge and better aspect ratio to the water.

6. When the yacht is sailing hard and is well heeled (this usually indicates that she would do better with a reef) the weather keel starts to break surface with heavy 'k'flumps' under the bilge. These thuds may irritate but are not in the least harmful and are no worse than those experienced under the weather chine of a V-bottom yacht when hard pressed.

7. Like the deep-fixed keel of a conventional deep-draught yacht the bilge keels are fixed and cannot be retracted to reduce surface friction resistance when sailing with the wind abaft the beam.

CENTREBOARDS

Advantages

1. The same benefits of cruising with shoal draught apply.

2. In light head winds the comparatively long leading edge of the fully lowered centreboard or plate is highly efficient in reducing leeway. The longer and deeper the CB the more effective it is.

3. With wind abaft the beam the CB can be hauled right up and its skin friction avoided. This is a notable feature when racing.

4. In varying wind conditions (from light airs to fresh winds) adjusting the angle of the CB can often affect the yacht's trim and helm angle to her advantage. This is also useful when racing.

5. When approaching shoals the CB scraping on the bottom is an instant and accurate sounding device.

6. If the yacht comes to a halt with the CB in the mud, hauling up the board smartly will often allow the yacht to be sailed off, even on the ebb.

7. When conditions at sea are becoming extreme (above Force 8) and a small yacht is no longer able to sail or carry any of her canvas, she may be forced to be left to lie ahull (under bare poles). Provided there is sea-room to leeward a centre-boarder will usually lie more safely and easily if her CB is hauled up. One of the greatest advantages of shallow draught has been shown countless times under these conditions, for as the yacht sidles to leeward, leaving a smooth or slick to wind-ward of her, advancing seas tend to break short of her and do not overwhelm her as they can a deep boat held firmly in the water.

8. With light draught a yacht in these conditions rides the leeward running surface water, where the keel of a deep boat will reach into the still water which tends to trip her into a capsize or stern-over-bow somersault.

Disadvantages

1. Installing a properly designed CB and its case adds con-siderably to the cost of a yacht.

2. A badly constructed case and faulty CB design can lead to familiar troubles with the board and leaks in the case.

3. In many CB yachts the case unnecessarily takes up valuable space in the cabin. With a careful design, however, this need not be, and the projecting part of the case can be utilized to form a fore-and-aft bulkhead for, say, the galley or lavatory compartment.

4. When the yacht has sat on the ground for several tides the board usually becomes jammed up in the case with mud, sand, shells or stones. If disadvantage 2 above applies and the designer has made no provision for opening up the top of the case while the yacht is afloat in order to free the board, it may remain stuck up until the yacht can be hauled out on a slip.

5. A steel centreplate, if too thin or old and reduced by rust, can get bent on striking the ground or when beating in a heavy

sea. Slipping the yacht and replacement of the buckled plate is the only remedy. The same trouble can also result if the CB has no stop to prevent it from swinging right down should the lifting tackle part or some clot let it go with a run.

*

Then, after all these pros and cons, which of the two types of boat really is the better? A good question, but there is patently no simple answer and only the individual owner can decide for himself whether he would find a bilge keel boat or a centre-boarder the more suited to his own needs.

Whereas twin bilge keels have appeared comparatively recently on the yachting scene – in any numbers within the past 20 years – drop keels, either sliding or pivoted, are a far older contrivance: they have been in the western world just about 200 years, but in China and India sliding drop keels were in use centuries before that. That well-designed centreboard yachts can be very fast indeed has been demonstrated many times. Some of the early successful defenders of the America's Cup were broad and shallow CB yachts which had no difficulty in outsailing the challenging deep-draught English cutters. In recent years Richard Nye's American-built centreboarder *Carina* astonished diehard English yachtsmen when she sailed across the Atlantic and won the Fastnet Cup against our stiffest R.O.R.C. competition. Not long after this Carleton Mitchell's Sparkman and Stephens-designed centreboarder *Finisterre* not only outsailed yachts in races in this country, but back home in his Long Island Sound waters Mitchell put up his first season's racing record as 23 firsts and three places out of 26 starts – and *Finisterre* is a very shallow-draught yacht with considerable beam.

For reasons of gain by reducing the wetted-surface resistance when running before the wind the moderate draught yacht with a sophisticated arrangement of drop or retractable keel – a fully streamlined heavy metal centreboard, in short – appears to be returning to British yacht racing, unless rules are devised to prevent this costly form of competition. For those yachtsmen, whether they race or cruise, who do own a yacht with a centre-board of wood or metal, and are worried about worm getting at the inside of the CB case, here is a useful tip, although a very old one: once or twice a season while the boat is afloat pour a gallon or two of paraffin (kerosene) or old sump oil into the case. The oil, being lighter than water, will float on the surface inside the case. Let the yacht settle on the ground on the ebb, and as the water drops the oil will thoroughly plaster the whole of the inside of the case and the board itself. This treatment not only deters wood borers but it helps to make the board work more smoothly and with less friction.

Only a few years now remained before the date when I should reach retiring age. With the enormous growth of all aspects of the yachting industry, a steady increase in the *Yachting Monthly*'s circulation, and additional work in connection with the build-yourself designs side, I found my time more and more taken up at weekends. Like so many other professional men all the signs indicated that for me my work would go on increasing as one grew older and slower, instead of tailing off as it used to do in grandfather's day. *Lone Gull* accordingly began to spend too much of her time on her mooring at Hardway, waiting in vain for us to be able to join her. The harsh economics of keeping an 8-tonner on the South Coast with so little spare time to sail her could not be ignored any longer, and very reluctantly we decided we had to part with this grand little ship.

Happily she went to an enthusiastic young fellow, Nicholas, who nursed a passion for cruising singlehanded, and would base her in East Scotland on the Fife coast within reach of his work. He loved her dearly from the first, and it was gratifying to know that she was in such appreciative and capable hands. During the years that Nicholas owned her, before he married and started a family and had perforce to relinquish the cruising life, he wrote us charming letters on his cruises, full of praise for the way *Lone Gull* behaved. And he certainly covered many leagues of rough waters in her. After collecting her in Portsmouth Harbour he sailed her, alone most of the way, up to the Firth of Forth. From there, during successive holidays from his work he cruised in her, again almost always entirely alone, southward along the East Coast to Dover and westward to visit his old home in the Channel Isles.

On visiting the Brittany coast he wrote that he found *Lone Gull* the ideal type of boat for such cruising, for while she was a fine dry boat with an easy motion at sea, and could be left to sail herself for hours on end, her shallow draught enabled her to get into harbours over a bar long before deeper-draught yachts could enter on the tide. And in harbours that dried out at low water, while the deep-keel yachts had fun and games rigging masthead guys and springs to keep from falling over away from the quay as the tide left them, *Lone Gull* sat happily on her bilge keels in a much less crowded part of the harbour with no risk of falling over. Thence from the Channel Isles Nicholas, on his own again, took his little ship up the West Coast to the Clyde, where she was left to spend the winter. When she again changed hands she returned to the East Coast, later to be based on the River Tay.

On the whole I think in *Lone Gull* II a fairly satisfactory design was arrived at which has proved itself well-suited to offshore cruising singlehanded or family boating; certainly owners of other boats built to this design in Australia, East Africa, Canada, Fiji as well as in England have praised their all-round qualities. The Amateur Yacht Research Society also paid the design the compliment of featuring it as the best of the year for the purpose of singlehanded offshore cruising. But simple bilge keels designed to withstand all the hard shocks of rough-and-tumble cruising, whether they are of $\frac{1}{2}$ in. steel-flanged plate or hydrofoil-shaped hardwood in planks through-bolted, cannot be as efficient in reducing leeway under all conditions as the conventional deep hydrofoil-sectioned ballast keel.

In the A.Y.R.S. review of the design Dr John Morwood, principal of the Society, wrote:

'It is possible that bilge keels could be designed to provide lateral resistance efficiently while not losing their value as sheerlegs. All that is necessary is to make both the leading and trailing edges of the bilge keels into hydrofoils with an aspect ratio of 3:1 and join the free ends with a metal rod which will prevent "end losses" at the after one. The four short hydrofoils will then provide a lot of lateral resistance for their area and not

188

turbulate the water so much. It will be far easier to clean inside them, the yacht will be faster on all courses and she will still be able to sit upright on the mud. *Lone Gull* II may be the utmost in sailing hydrodynamic efficiency and sea kindliness while at the same time giving the greatest amount of accommodation for the cost. A method for designing more efficient bilge keels is suggested.'

Understandably the current cost of building these boats of good materials and with good workmanship, which was then in the region of £5,000 to £6,000, has prevented their being produced in any quantity, and further research into design improvements was prevented by other events. During a period of revolutionary changes in the press world, of takeover bids, mergers, liquidation, and changes in employment, I was unable to follow up this interesting lead, and indeed I little thought at that time that seven more years would elapse ere I should be able to have once again a little ship of my own, seven somewhat empty years so far as messing about in boats was concerned.

Not long before my retirement date was due the *Yachting Monthly*, which had been an independent concern since it was started in 1906, was taken over by a giant publishing corporation with many ramifications in the printing and press world, and over thirty thousand employees on its roll. As with nearly all takeovers many minor alterations in work followed, the readership of yachting magazines and the whole yachting scene were changing, there appeared to be more paperwork than ever, and after a run with the old company of something over 40 years I felt sad to part from old colleagues, but not averse to hand over the wheel to Des Sleightholme, a capable and younger skipper.

Looking back over the years it warms the heart to think that the long row of issues of the *Yachting Monthly* when I was Editor – over four hundred of them – have given pleasure to so many readers, that my various books have brought me many friends, and that by now there are well over 1600 little yachts built to my designs which are sailing with contented owners and families in many parts of the world. There is more time to give

189

to writing and design work, opportunity for long-awaited travel, and with a mooring laid at a charming spot on the Deben River within walking distance of our house, Marjorie and I should be content. And what kind of boat will be the successor to *Lone Gull* II? That I suppose could be another story.

INDEX

Index

Yachts referred to in text